A PRACTICAL GUIDE TO MENTAL HEALTH LAW

The Mental Health Act 1983 and related legislation

Larry Gostin

Foreword by Lady Bingley   *Edited by* Janet Manning

© MIND 1983

Published by MIND (National Association for Mental Health)
22 Harley Street, London W1N 2ED

ISBN 0 900557 59 1

Designed by David Burton & Associates, London

Printed in England by G Donald & Company Limited

ACKNOWLEDGEMENTS

A Practical Guide to Mental Health Law represents the culmination of a decade of intense concern within MIND, and it is dedicated to the people who have fought long and hard to promote the rights and status of mentally ill and mentally handicapped people. The landmarks in the process of change – **A Human Condition**, *X v The United Kingdom* and the voting rights cases – could not have been achieved without the full support and invaluable contribution of members of MIND's Council of Management and staff. In the early days the most notable proponents of legal and welfare rights included David Ennals, Juliet Bingley, Derek Russell Davis, Tony Smythe, Tessa Jowell and Ron Lacey. More recently, the task of following the Mental Health Bill through Parliament was accomplished with energy and expertise by William Bingley. To members of the House of Commons Standing Committee on the Bill, and to the DHSS staff who worked intelligently and tirelessly, goes our admiration. For detailed assistance with the preparation of this book I warmly thank Laura Jacobs; for administrative work, Hazel Burke; for secretarial skill, Margaret Windsor. For fulsome support and energy I owe a particular debt of gratitude to Chris Heginbotham.

This is a time when old alliances must be cemented, and differences of opinion set aside, in the cause of a constructive approach to the new legislation. We thank our friends at BASW – Rolf Olsen, John Cypher and Molly Meacher; at the Royal College of Psychiatrists – Kenneth Rawnsley, Gerald Timbury and Robert Bluglass; at the Royal College of Nursing – Peter Mellor; and at COHSE – the late Albert Spanswick for joining with us in seeking the reform of the Mental Health Act 1959.

Finally – but most important in personal terms – my thanks go as ever to my wife Jean.

Larry Gostin
Oxford, July 1983

FOREWORD

In many ways the Mental Health Act 1983 owes its genesis to MIND and in particular to two men—Tony Smythe, who was appointed MIND's National Director in 1974, and Larry Gostin who joined MIND as its first Legal Officer in the same year, having just completed a Fulbright Scholarship at Oxford University. He subsequently became Legal Director. These appointments heralded a radical shift in both the objectives and the style of MIND: one of the organisation's primary concerns became the reform of the Mental Health Act 1959 in order to increase the rights of compulsorily detained patients.

The process by which this organisational aim saw fulfilment in the 1983 Act was precipitated by the publication in 1975 of both the report of the Committee on Mentally Abnormal Offenders (the Butler Report) and the first volume of **A Human Condition** by Larry Gostin. MIND can be justly proud of the fact that two-thirds of the new provisions in the 1983 Act are based on proposals originally made in **A Human Condition**. These provisions include—

- the reduction in the periods of compulsory detention
- the 'treatability' test
- the right of restricted patients to apply to a Mental Health Review Tribunal for discharge
- automatic reviews by tribunals
- tribunals for patients detained for assessment
- greater legal safeguards for patients transferred from prison to hospital
- improved training and qualifications for social workers with responsibilities conferred by the Mental Health Act
- clarification of a detained patient's right to withhold consent to treatment (although MIND still has some reservations about this particular part of the new Act).

From the mid-70s on, pressure for changes in the Mental Health Act 1959 was exerted by MIND and other concerned organisations. MIND itself liaised extensively with bodies such as the Royal College of Psychiatrists and with the governments of the day. All this activity culminated in the publication of the Mental Health (Amendment) Bill at the end of 1981, and MIND then identified the key areas on which it would focus attention.

To a great extent many of the measures now on the statute book represent the successful conclusion of campaigns waged by MIND over many years. Major issues of particular significance for MIND were these—

EXTENSION OF VOTING RIGHTS

MIND has pressed long and hard for informal patients in psychiatric and mental handicap hospitals to have the right to vote—just as patients in general hospitals have. Indeed, the very first test case ever brought by MIND's Legal Department concerned voting rights for patients in psychiatric hospitals. On 15 June 1976 the County Court made a major decision in the case of *Wild and Others v The Electoral Registration Officer for Warrington* which gave mentally ill patients the right to vote if they were in hospital solely because they had no home to go to. With this very much in mind, staff at Calderstones Hospital in Lancashire asked the Clitheroe Electoral Registration Officer to enfranchise 618 of their mentally handicapped residents on the grounds that these people were only in hospital because there was no alternative provision for them in the community. The application was turned down in March 1981, so three of the residents, again represented by MIND, appealed successfully to the County Court.

During its discussions on the Amendment Bill, the House of Commons Special Standing Committee agreed that *all* informal patients should have the right to vote. Unfortunately, due to Parliamentary pressures this decision was not implemented in full: informal patients now have the right to vote, but still cannot use the hospital as a residential address for electoral purposes. These provisions are now confirmed in the Representation of the People Act 1983.

ACCESS TO THE COURTS

Section 141 of the 1959 Act severely restricted the right of mental patients to bring a criminal or civil action against hospital staff. **A Human Condition** emphasised the limitations of this section and MIND subsequently brought two cases on the subject before the European Commission of Human Rights.

MIND also helped bring the *Pountney v Griffiths* case to the House of Lords in 1975, arguing that patients should have an absolute right to sue in certain circumstances. It was therefore particularly pleasing that a substantial amendment was passed at the Committee Stage of the Bill, reforming section 141 and removing the protection this section previously afforded the Secretary of State and the health authorities.

THE MENTAL HEALTH ACT COMMISSION

The proposal to establish a Mental Health Act Commission was put formally by the Royal College of Psychiatrists, although the Commission differs remarkably little from the Committee on the Rights and Responsibilities of Staff and Residents of Psychiatric Hospitals (CORR) mooted in **A Human Condition**. MIND supported Commons moves to make the Commission a significantly stronger body, especially the proposal that it should publish annual reports.

THE EUROPEAN COURT OF HUMAN RIGHTS

MIND originally launched the case of *X v The United Kingdom* in 1974, and the European Court of Human Rights finally decided in MIND's favour on 5 November 1981. The case involved a patient who was recalled to Broadmoor by the Home Secretary following a matrimonial dispute, and in a landmark decision the European Court ruled that patients detained under restriction orders must have the right to a court hearing. The English writ of *habeas corpus* is not sufficient. Following the Court's ruling, the Government published a critically important set of amendments to ensure that the new legislation would comply fully with the Court's decision, and the 1983 Act now gives Mental Health Review Tribunals the authority to discharge restricted patients.

EXCLUSION OF MENTAL HANDICAP FROM PART IV OF THE MENTAL HEALTH ACT 1959

MIND originally made the proposal to exclude mental handicap from Part IV of the Mental Health Act 1959 in an article published in **APEX,** the journal of the Institute of Mental Subnormality, in 1978. In the event, the actual amendment embodied in the new Act was initiated in the House of Lords by Lord Renton, Chairman of Mencap. This amendment replaced the term *subnormality* (which was used throughout the 1959 Act) by *mental impairment,* and should mean that most mentally handicapped people are excluded from the long-term detention provisions of the new Act.

EXTENSION OF LEGAL AID TO COVER REPRESENTATION AT MENTAL HEALTH REVIEW TRIBUNALS

For many years MIND has operated a representation service for patients appearing before Mental Health Review Tribunals (MHRTs), and has urged successive Governments to extend legal aid to cover this special kind of representation. Oral and written representations were made to the Lord Chancellor's Advisory Committee, the Law Society, the Council on Tribunals and the Royal Commission on Legal Services, and each of these bodies subsequently joined MIND in advocating the extension of legal aid. It was therefore bitterly disappointing that an amendment to extend legal aid should be defeated in the House of Lords by just two votes. However, when the Bill reached the Commons the Government finally acceded to mounting public pressure and extended Assistance by Way of Representation to Mental Health Review Tribunals. In practical terms this was one of the most important changes effected during the passage of the Bill through Parliament, and one which enjoyed the support of members of all political parties.

APPROVED SOCIAL WORKERS

MIND has long supported BASW and other organisations in urging more stringent safeguards and training for social workers involved in duties conferred by the Mental Health Act. We were therefore particularly pleased with the provisions in the new Act relating to approved social workers, and regard this as potentially one of the most exciting developments in the new legislation.

DUTIES OF SOCIAL SERVICES DEPARTMENTS

In **A Human Condition** MIND stated uncompromisingly that its objective for the next decade was to 'provide a legal framework for community psychiatry'. It was therefore deeply gratifying that the House of Lords should have voted an amendment imposing on social services departments a mandatory duty to provide after-care for certain categories of detained patients when they are discharged. MIND would naturally have preferred that this provision had been extended to all discharged patients needing after-care, but hopefully the provision will at the very least highlight the lamentable shortage of resources in this area.

CONSENT TO TREATMENT

Consent to treatment was the most controversial legislative issue before the publication of the Bill, and continued to be so during the Bill's passage through Parliament. MIND made its position on consent clear in an article published in the **Journal of the Royal Society of Medicine** in October 1981, and joined the DHSS and the Royal College of Psychiatrists for a series of meetings to thrash out a compromise approach to the issue. In formulating the new legislation the Government made a sincere and highly professional attempt to reconcile the disparate views of MIND and the College. Many of MIND's basic principles have been adopted, notably multidisciplinary review in consultation, but there is still much with which MIND must remain dissatisfied. In a lengthy letter published in the **British Medical Journal** on 26 June 1982, Larry Gostin and Professor Derek Russell Davis stated MIND's view that the new legislation is overly legalistic in form and procedure, but nonetheless provides insufficient safeguards. MIND's priority in the coming years will be to ensure that the Mental Health Act Commission helps make the new provisions more effective and accessible to patients.

The Mental Health Act 1983 is the product of the concern and care of many individuals and organisations. Their achievement must be acknowledged, and tribute must also be paid to the Government which found Parliamentary time for this important measure during 1981 and 1982, and to the previous administration which devoted considerable time and energy to formulating the basis of many provisions subsequently incorporated in the new legislation.

New laws are frequently as effective and innovative as the people who put them into practice want them to be. I hope that this guide will provide a firm foundation of knowledge and practical support for every person, be they patient or professional, who wants to use the new legislation to effect real and beneficial changes in our attitude towards mental ill-health and how we cope with it.

Lady Bingley
Chairman of MIND

PREFACE

Many of the principles which shape current mental health legislation were established by the Royal Commission on the Law relating to Mental Illness and Mental Deficiency, chaired by Lord Percy. The Royal Commission reported in 1957, and the Mental Health Act 1959 was based almost entirely upon its recommendations. The 1959 Act swept away much of the legalistic framework of the old Lunacy Laws passed between 1890 and 1930: it was guided by the philosophy that, whenever possible, care should be provided without the use of compulsion; informal admission for psychiatric treatment should be in no way different from admission to hospital for the medical treatment of physical illness; and the use of compulsion, when necessary, should be subject in the first instance to primarily professional discretion. It also established that an administrative tribunal with a medical member should be responsible for reviewing medical decision-making.

The Mental Health Act 1959 stood virtually unamended until the Mental Health (Amendment) Act 1982 was enacted on 28 October 1982. The provisions of the 1959 and 1982 Acts were consolidated in the Mental Health Act 1983 which stands today as a comprehensive piece of mental health legislation affecting the lives of all mentally disordered people in hospital. It is a tribute to the legislators who designed the 1959 Act that many of the fundamental principles upon which it was originally based have been left intact. Undoubtedly, the most significant change in the law is to give mental patients greater protection where the use of compulsion is involved. The process of reforming the 1959 Act began in 1975 with the publication of MIND's **A Human Condition** and of the report of the Committee on Mentally Abnormal Offenders, which was chaired by Lord Butler. A Consultative Document was published in 1976, followed by a White Paper in 1978. A further explanatory White Paper was then published together with the Mental Health (Amendment) Bill in November 1981.

This guide aims to offer a practical explanation of current mental health legislation to workers who provide the services, consumers who use them, and others who are interested in the welfare of mentally disordered people. Some of the text first appeared in the **New Law Journal** (2, 9 and 23 December 1982), and MIND wishes to thank the publishers for permission to reproduce it here. Readers who require more detail than this guide is intended to provide are advised to consult L.O. Gostin, **Mental Health Services and the Law** (5th edition) (London, Shaw & Sons, 1984).

The information in this guide reflects the legislative position in England and Wales, *not* that in Scotland or Northern Ireland.

Larry Gostin
Visiting Fellow in Psychiatry and Law,
Oxford University, Centre for Criminological Research
Legal Director, MIND 1974-83

KEY TO ABBREVIATIONS

ASW	approved social worker
DHSS	Department of Health and Social Security
ECT	electroconvulsive therapy
MHAC	Mental Health Act Commission
MHRT	Mental Health Review Tribunal
MWO	mental welfare officer
RMO	responsible medical officer
s	section (unless otherwise indicated, section numbers refer to the Mental Health Act 1983)

CONTENTS

CHAPTER 8
THE MENTAL HEALTH ACT COMMISSION

CHAPTER 9
IN-PATIENT RIGHTS

CHAPTER 10
THE ROLE OF THE HOSPITAL MANAGERS

CHAPTER 1

INTRODUCTORY CONCEPTS: DEFINITIONS, INFORMAL ADMISSION & HOLDING POWERS

MENTAL DISORDER AND RELATED DEFINITIONS

Mental disorder is defined in the Mental Health Act 1983 as 'mental illness, arrested or incomplete development of mind, psychopathic disorder and any other disorder or disability of mind' (s1(2)). The phrase 'any other disorder or disability of mind' gives the umbrella term *mental disorder* a wide meaning, potentially encompassing a broad range of behaviour. However, the Act stipulates that a person may not be classified as mentally disordered 'by reason only of promiscuity or other immoral conduct, sexual deviancy or dependence on alcohol or drugs' (s1(3)).

Four categories of mental disorder are specified – mental illness, severe mental impairment, mental impairment and psychopathic disorder – and it is helpful to sub-divide these four categories into major and minor disorders because different legal consequences may ensue from the classification of disorder. The *major* forms of mental disorder are mental illness and severe mental impairment; because they are considered to be major disorders they do not generally carry a *treatability* requirement as part of the criteria for long-term compulsory admission. The *minor* disorders are mental impairment and psychopathic disorder; because these are held to be less serious forms of mental disorder the Act requires that they must be *treatable* before a person can be compulsorily admitted to hospital for a long period. Under the terms of the Mental Health Act 1959 there were age limits attached to compulsory admission for treatment in the case of a person suffering from a minor disorder; these age limits have been abolished by the 1983 Act.

The definitions of mental disorder and the forms of mental disorder specified in the 1983 Act are *legal* classifications to be used for the purposes of the law. They should not be confused with *medical* terminology, which has no particular legal significance. For example, mental illness is a specific classification under the Mental Health Act, whereas schizophrenia and depression are medical diagnoses which are established through professional training and experience; terms like these do not appear in mental health legislation.

The four legal classifications of mental disorder are discussed below. It is the doctor's responsibility, where appropriate, to classify the disorder in each individual case. The patient's responsible medical officer or a Mental Health Review Tribunal may subsequently decide that *he is suffering from a different form of mental disorder and reclassify him accordingly (ss16, 72).

MENTAL ILLNESS

Mental illness is a sub-category of mental disorder, but is not defined in the Act. It is the only specific form of disorder which is not defined.

SEVERE MENTAL IMPAIRMENT

Severe mental impairment means 'a state of arrested or incomplete development of mind which includes severe impairment of intelligence and social functioning and is associated with abnormally aggressive or seriously irresponsible conduct' (s1(2)).

MENTAL IMPAIRMENT

The term *mental impairment* is defined in exactly the same way as severe mental impairment, except that it encompasses 'significant' (as opposed to 'severe') impairment of intelligence and social functioning (s1(2)). The legal difference between the terms *severe* and *significant* is by no means clear, reflecting only a subtle difference in emphasis.

PSYCHOPATHIC DISORDER

Psychopathic disorder means 'a persistent disorder or disability of mind (whether or not including significant impairment of intelligence) which results in abnormally aggressive or seriously irresponsible conduct' (s1(2)).

CHANGES FROM THE 1959 ACT

The term *subnormality* which was used in the 1959 Act has been replaced by *mental impairment* in the new Act, but this does not mean that mental handicap has been removed from the scope of mental health legislation. The general definition of mental disorder still refers to 'arrested or incomplete development of mind', and this can be taken to encompass mental handicap. Thus, wherever the generic term *mental disorder* is used in health or social services legislation, it includes mental handicap. Mentally handicapped people will still be eligible for all services specified in legislation including priority housing, care and after-care. They will also continue to be liable to be detained for up to 28 days for assessment or for up to 72 hours (ie emergency admission) if appropriate. They may also be subject to the jurisdiction of the Court of Protection.

In legal terms, however, the effect of the 1983 Act will be to remove the great majority of mentally handicapped people from the scope of those provisions which require that a person must be suffering from one of the four specific categories of mental disorder. Therefore mentally handicapped people will *not* be subject to compulsory admission to hospital for treatment, reception into

---

The masculine pronoun is used throughout the Mental Health Act 1983. For convenience and clarity it will also be used in this guide.

guardianship, admission under a hospital order (with or without restrictions), or an order or transfer direction with the same effect as a hospital order *unless* their condition is associated with *abnormally aggressive or seriously irresponsible conduct.*

For the purposes of the law and of hospital records, the great majority of mentally handicapped people should be legally classified as suffering from *arrested or incomplete development of mind.* For medical or nursing purposes, however, and in common language, the term *mentally handicapped* should be retained. Only if a mentally handicapped person is dangerous or seriously irresponsible in his conduct should he be classified as mentally impaired.

In sum, mentally handicapped people can no longer be compulsorily admitted to hospital for long periods unless they exhibit seriously irresponsible or abnormally aggressive behaviour. For most other purposes, however, they are still subject to the provisions of the Mental Health Act and related legislation.

SOME OBSERVATIONS ON THE FORMS OF MENTAL DISORDER DEFINED IN THE ACT

The common feature of the three forms of mental disorder defined in the Act (ie mental impairment, severe mental impairment and psychopathic disorder) is that they all include *abnormally aggressive* or *seriously irresponsible* conduct. As each may also include impairment of intelligence, the three defined categories are remarkably similar in scope and implied objective.

The removal of the majority of mentally handicapped people from the scope of the provisions relating to long term detention goes some way towards satisfying those who claimed that the Act is inappropriate for this group of people. Nevertheless the inclusion of mentally handicapped people in *any* of the provisions relating to detention implies that mental handicap, like mental illness, is a temporary disorder which may be alleviated or cured by treatment. This is not so. Mental handicap is currently understood as a *permanent* disability which is detectable from an early age and is often associated with genetic or perinatal damage. The sudden onset and temporary or recurrent nature of mental illness are not characteristic of mental handicap. Mental handicap cannot be cured, but behavioural problems associated with the handicap may be significantly improved by training, education, socialisation and appropriate care. Concern has also been expressed that the label *mental impairment* (like *psychopathic disorder)* is likely to become stigmatic and therefore harmful.

Turning to psychopathic disorder itself, it should be noted that the clinical concept of this disorder has been interpreted in highly diverse ways. It sometimes has been taken to include minor forms of personality disorder and inadequacies of various descriptions, for example sexual deviancy or addiction to drugs or alcohol. However, the phrase 'persistent disorder', which is the legal definition, is significant. It denotes that the disorder must be a long-standing one; a person who has committed an isolated offence or displayed aggressive or irresponsible conduct on one occasion only cannot be categorised as psychopathic under the Act. In practice, psychopathic disorder is not regarded as a specific clinical condition; rather the presence of the disorder is inferred from evidence of anti-social behaviour. Thus the definition is a tautological one in that it implies a disorder originating from anti-social behaviour, while purporting to explain the behaviour *by* the presence of the disorder. As a result the label *psychopathic* has

3

been applied to a wide variety of people who have nothing in common except some sort of anti-social behaviour. There is no clear, consistent and rational distinction between offenders who are labelled psychopaths and sent by the courts to hospital and habitual offenders who are sent to prison without any psychiatric label.

The Committee on Mentally Abnormal Offenders (the Butler Committee) (Cmnd 6244, 1975) concluded that psychiatry was unable to provide any effective treatment for psychopathic disorder. The 1983 Act therefore restricts the admission of psychopathic patients under provisions relating to long term detention to cases where treatment is expected to benefit the patient or prevent a deterioration of his condition. In view of the findings of the Butler Committee, it is to be expected that the burden of demonstrating that the disorder is treatable will fall upon the hospital authorities; they should justify a specific treatment programme with clear behavioural goals and establish time periods within which those goals must be met.

RELATED DEFINITIONS

PATIENT

A *patient* is defined as 'a person suffering or appearing to be suffering from mental disorder' (s145). Thus, for the purposes of the Mental Health Act, a patient need only be *appearing* to suffer from mental disorder (not necessarily any specific form of disorder). The term *patient* does not only refer to people in hospital. For the purposes of Part VII of the Act, the term *patient* takes on a different meaning, referring to a person who in under the jurisdiction of the Court of Protection (s94).

MEDICAL TREATMENT

Medical treatment, the Act states, 'includes nursing, and also includes care, habilitation and rehabilitation under medical supervision' (s145). The term is therefore defined quite widely to encompass activities undertaken by nurses, psychologists, occupational therapists and other professionals – although these must all be under *medical supervision* if they are to be legally classified as medical treatment.

HOSPITAL

A *hospital* is 'any health service hospital within the meaning of the National Health Service Act 1977; and any accommodation provided by a local authority and used as a hospital by or on behalf of the Secretary of State under that Act' (s145). Accordingly, mentally disordered people may be admitted to general hospitals as well as mental illness or mental handicap hospitals, or special hospitals. They can also be admitted to mental nursing homes which are registered under the Nursing Homes Act 1975, although a mental nursing home cannot accept patients compulsorily admitted under Part III of the 1983 Act unless it is registered for that purpose under section 3(4)(b) of the 1975 Act (s34) (See also Health and Social Services and Social Security Adjudications Act 1983, s11 schedule 4). Any private or voluntary hospital or home which admits mentally disordered people *must* be registered as a mental nursing home.

SPECIAL HOSPITAL

A *special hospital* is a hospital established for people who are subject to detention under the Mental Health Act and who, in the opinion of the Secretary of State for Social Services, require treatment under conditions of special security because of their 'dangerous, violent or criminal propensities' (National Health Service Act 1977, s4). At the moment there are four special hospitals for England and Wales: Broadmoor (Crowthorne, Berkshire), Rampton (Retford, Nottinghamshire), Moss Side and Park Lane (both on the same site in Maghull, near Liverpool). Special hospitals are maintained to treat detained patients, and informal patients should not be admitted to them. Unlike other hospitals, they are managed directly by the Secretary of State for Social Services. An Office Committee (Special Hospitals) in the DHSS exercises most management functions on behalf of the Secretary of State.

REGIONAL SECURE UNIT

Regional secure units are intended to meet the particular needs of people who require a service which falls somewhere between that offered by local mental illness or mental handicap hospitals and the special hospitals. An interim report by the Butler Committee in 1974 recommended that regional secure units should be established in each Regional Health Authority area, but they have no formal statutory basis in law.

There have been considerable difficulties in setting up these units, and there are only a few in operation. For a fuller description of regional secure units see chapter 9 of **A Human Condition** (volume 2) (MIND, 1977).

THE MANAGERS

The definition of the term *managers* varies according to the facility in question—
- in relation to a NHS hospital or local authority accommodation used as a hospital, the *managers* are the District Health Authority or special health authority responsible for the administration of the hospital;
- in relation to a special hospital, the term *managers* indicates the Secretary of State for Social Services;
- in relation to a mental nursing home, the *managers* means the person(s) registered in respect of that home (s145).

The managers have a number of specific responsibilities under the Mental Health Act 1983. These are described in chapter 10.

INFORMAL ADMISSION TO HOSPITAL

The Royal Commission on the Law relating to Mental Illness and Mental Deficiency, which reported in 1957, recommended that mentally disordered patients should be admitted to hospital on the same basis as people who are receiving treatment for a physical illness. Accordingly it proposed that there should be no special forms or certificates to be signed, no proof that a patient had given a valid consent to admission, and no requirement that he should give notice of his intention to leave hospital. It suggested that *informal* admission should replace *voluntary* admission which then existed under the terms of the Lunacy Act 1890 together with the Mental Treatment Act 1930. The significance of informal admission is that a person need not express positive willingness to be admitted to hospital; it is sufficient that he is not *unwilling* to be admitted. Thus, informal admission allows the 'non-volitional' or 'non-protesting' patient to be treated in hospital without the use of formal compulsory powers. If a person agrees to enter hospital on an informal basis, it would normally be improper to use compulsory powers under the Act.

The introduction of informal admission has triggered a revolution in the philosophy of care for people who are mentally disordered. Approximately 90 per cent of all admissions today are informal, and 94 per cent of current hospital residents were admitted on an informal basis.

LEGAL POSITION OF INFORMAL PATIENTS

Section 131 is the only provision in the Act which relates to informal admission. It states—

> 'Nothing in this Act shall be construed as preventing a patient who requires treatment for mental disorder from being admitted to any hospital or mental nursing home in pursuance of arrangements made in that behalf and without any application, order or direction rendering him liable to be detained under this Act, or from remaining in any hospital or mental nursing home in pursuance of such arrangements after he has ceased to be so liable to be detained' (s131(1)).

It is generally thought that a minor under the age of 16 can be informally admitted to hospital on the authority of his parent or guardian. A minor who has passed his 16th birthday and is capable of expressing his own wishes can admit himself to hospital informally 'notwithstanding any right of custody or control vested by law in his parent or guardian' (s131(2)). It appears, therefore, that the parents of a competent minor aged 16 or older cannot prevent him from admitting himself to hospital informally if a consultant is willing to provide a bed.

Informal patients are free to leave hospital at any time subject to the *holding powers* or *common law powers* described on pp 7-9. In most instances, therefore, it is unlawful to prevent an informal patient from leaving hospital if he wishes to do so – for example by locking the hospital ward, seclusion or physical restraint.

In nearly every respect the legal position of informal psychiatric patients is the same as that of non-psychiatric patients. Most significantly, informal patients enjoy the ordinary common law right to refuse treatment. The Mental Health (Amendment) Act 1982 removed two of the restrictions on the rights of informal patients which existed under the 1959 Act – the withholding of post and the removal of alien patients from the United Kingdom. In addition, the legal position of informal patients in relation to electoral registration has been strengthened. The Amendment Act did not expressly exclude informal patients from the provisions now embodied in section 139 of the 1983 Act (formerly section 141 of the 1959 Act), as recommended in the 1978 White Paper. Section 139 concerns the patient's right of access to a court. However, in *R v Runighian [1977] Criminal Law Review 361,* the Warwick Crown Court held that section 141 of the 1959 Act was not applicable to informal patients, at least in the circumstances presented in that case (an alleged assault by a nurse).

For a full description of the law on these issues as it applies to informal patients, see the relevant section of this guide.

APPLICATION IN RESPECT OF PATIENTS ALREADY IN HOSPITAL

An application for compulsory admission to hospital under Part II of the 1983 Act can be made 'notwithstanding that the patient is already an in-patient in that hospital' (s5(1)). As long as the proper procedures are observed an informal patient can therefore be compulsorily admitted to hospital for assessment or treatment in the same way as any person in the community.

Certain doctors and nurses have special holding powers which can be brought to bear in respect of patients who are already in hospital.

DOCTOR'S HOLDING POWER

Statutory authority: ss5(2) – 5(3)

Maximum duration of detention: 72 hours

Criterion: an application for compulsory admission 'ought to be made'

Procedure: the medical practitioner in charge of treatment (or his designate) furnishes a report to the hospital managers

If the medical practitioner in charge of treatment considers that an application for the compulsory admission of an informal patient 'ought to be made', he can furnish the managers with a written report to that effect. The patient can be detained for 72 hours 'from the time when the report is so furnished' (s5(2)).

The registered medical practitioner in charge of the patient's treatment may nominate one (but only one) other registered medical practitioner on the hospital staff to act for him in respect of this section (s5(3)).

The doctor's holding power can be exercised 'in the case of a patient who is an in-patient in a hospital'. Accordingly it can be used, provided the statutory criterion is satisfied, to compulsorily detain any in-patient, even one receiving treatment for a physical illness in a general hospital.

NURSE'S HOLDING POWER

Statutory authority: ss5(4) – 5(7)

Maximum duration of detention: six hours

Criterion: the patient appears to be suffering from mental disorder to such a degree that it is necessary for his health or safety, or the protection of others, for him to be immediately restrained from leaving the hospital; and it is not practicable to secure the immediate attendance of the medical practitioner in charge of treatment or his designate

Procedure: a first level nurse must record the fact in writing

If a nurse *of the prescribed class* (a first level nurse who is qualified in nursing mentally ill or mentally handicapped people, as defined in the Mental Health (Nurses) Order 1983 considers that a patient is mentally disordered to such a degree that it is necessary for his health or safety or for the protection of others for him to be immediately restrained from leaving the hospital, and that it is not practicable to secure the immediate attendance of the medical practitioner in charge of treatment or his designate, he can record that fact in writing. The record must be in the form prescribed in regulations. It must be delivered by the nurse (or a person authorised by the nurse) to the hospital managers. The nurse's record provides sufficient authority for the patient to be compulsorily detained for a period of six hours from the time of the recording or until the arrival of a practitioner with the authority to exercise a doctor's holding power, whichever is earlier. Once the medical practitioner has arrived in the place where the patient is detained the nurse's holding power lapses, even if the six hour period has not yet expired. The medical practitioner can then decide whether to furnish a report to the managers authorising the patient's detention for 72 hours; the six hour period counts as part of the 72 hours.

The nurse's holding power can only be exercised in the case of a patient who is receiving in-patient hospital treatment for mental disorder. It does not, therefore, apply to non-psychiatric patients in general hospitals.

COMMON LAW POWERS OF DETENTION

There may be occasions when there is no medical practitioner in charge of treatment (or a designate) and no first level nurse present on a hospital ward. If an emergency then arises, it may be necessary for ward staff to rely upon general common law powers which are not embodied in statute. In common law any individual is entitled to apprehend and restrain a person who is mentally disordered and who presents an imminent danger to himself or to others. It is therefore lawful for a nurse (or any other person) to apprehend and restrain a mentally disordered patient if there are reasonable grounds to believe that he poses a danger to himself or to others, or would do so if he were to leave the hospital. This could mean physically controlling the patient by bodily force or mechanical restraints or seclusion. Ward staff are well-advised to avoid the use of sedation without the patient's consent unless it is specifically prescribed by a qualified doctor. A nurse administering *PRN medication in such circumstances would have considerable difficulty in justifying its use without consent and/or without medical direction.

It must be emphasised that the scope of these common law powers of apprehension and restraint is limited. The degree of medical or physical intervention used should be sufficient to bring the emergency to an end, but no greater. Any method of restraint which involves excessive force, or which continues in use after the immediate crisis is over, is not justified under common law.

In summary then, when an emergency arises on a hospital ward and it is necessary to restrain an informal patient or to prevent him from leaving the hospital, it is preferable for a medical practitioner to exercise a 72 hour holding power by furnishing a report to the hospital managers. If neither the relevant doctor nor his designate is available, it may be necessary for a registered mental nurse to exercise a six hour holding power by making a record in the patient's notes. Failing the use of these holding powers, any individual is entitled to exercise his common law right to restrain a mentally disordered person who presents an imminent danger to himself or to others. However, these common law powers may not be used if there is *no* immediate danger but merely a general concern about the health of a patient. When they are used, the degree and duration of the force involved must be proportional to the risk which is presented.

PRN medication is any medication a doctor enters in a patient's records for possible use as and when circumstances dictate.

Where appropriate, the powers conferred by the Mental Health Act should be used in preference to those embodied in common law. By observing the provisions of the Act, a nurse has clearer authority for his action, and also enjoys the protection afforded by section 139 which relates to the patient's right of access to the courts.

CHAPTER 2

COMPULSORY ADMISSION TO HOSPITAL & GUARDIANSHIP PART II OF THE ACT

Part II of the Mental Health Act 1983 sets out the criteria and procedures for compulsory admission to hospital and guardianship. It covers various categories of admission including admission for assessment in cases of emergency for up to 72 hours (s4); admission for assessment for up to 28 days (s2); and admission for treatment for up to six months, renewable for a further six months and then for periods of one year at a time (s3). Part II also makes provision for reception into guardianship for periods of the same duration as those of admission for treatment (s7).

Part X of the Act (Miscellaneous Provisions) includes two sections which provide for compulsory detention for a period of up to 72 hours: warrant to search for and remove patients (s135), and mentally disordered persons found in public places (s136).

ADMISSION FOR ASSESSMENT IN CASES OF EMERGENCY

Statutory authority: s4

Maximum duration of detention: 72 hours

Criterion: it is of 'urgent necessity' for the patient to be detained, and compliance with the provisions for admission for assessment would involve 'undesirable delay'

Procedure: recommendation by one medical practitioner and an application by an approved social worker or the nearest relative

In a case of urgent necessity, an application for admission for assessment can be made by an approved social worker (ASW) or by the patient's *nearest* relative. The application must state that it is of 'urgent necessity' for the patient to be admitted and detained for assessment, and that compliance with the procedures for an admission for assessment under section 2 would involve 'undesirable delay'. The applicant must have personally seen the patient within the period of 24 hours before the application is made.

An emergency application under section 4 must be based on one medical recommendation, if practicable by a doctor who has previous knowledge of the patient (for example his general practitioner). This recommendation must verify the statement made in the application, and must be signed on or before the date of the application (s12). A patient must be admitted to hospital within a period of 24 hours starting from the time he is medically examined or the application is made, whichever is the earlier (s6(1)(b)).

An emergency admission ceases to have effect 72 hours after the patient is admitted to hospital *unless* the managers receive the medical recommendation required for admission for assessment within that period.

CHANGES FROM THE 1959 ACT

A substantial proportion of all compulsory admissions to hospital under the Mental Health Act 1959 was the result of emergency applications, which led to the criticism that emergency applications were being made in cases other than those of *urgent necessity*. In response to this criticism the Amendment Act 1982 made three significant changes: the period within which the applicant must have seen the patient was reduced from three days to 24 hours; the period within which the patient must be admitted to hospital following the medical examination or application (whichever is the earlier) was also reduced from three days to 24 hours; and the application had to be made by the *nearest* relative, as opposed to *any* relative.

ADMISSION FOR ASSESSMENT

Statutory authority: s2

Maximum duration of detention: 28 days

Criteria: (a) the patient is suffering from mental disorder of a nature or degree which warrants his detention in a hospital 'for assessment (or for assessment followed by medical treatment)' for at least a limited period; and
(b) he ought to be so detained in the interests of his own health or safety or with a view to the protection of others

Procedure: recommendation by two medical practitioners and an application by an approved social worker or the nearest relative

An application for admission for assessment must be made by an approved social worker or the patient's nearest relative (s11(1)). If an ASW makes the application he must, either before or within a reasonable time after the application is made, 'take such steps as are practicable' to inform the nearest relative that the application is to be or has been made, and that the nearest relative has the power to order the patient's discharge (s11(3)). (For discussion on the right of a nearest relative to discharge the patient, see p 29). Unlike the case of admission for treatment, there is no obligation on the approved social worker to consult with, and obtain the agreement of, the nearest relative before making an application for assessment.

The applicant must have personally seen the patient within a period of 14 days before the application is made (s11(5)).

An application for admission for assessment must be based on the written recommendations of two registered medical practitioners who must state that the relevant criteria are satisfied. Under the terms of section 12 of the Act, one of the practitioners must be approved by the Secretary of State for Social Services 'as having special experience in the diagnosis or treatment of mental disorder'. (For further information on medical recommendations, see pp.00.)

A patient admitted to hospital for assessment may be detained for a period of no longer than 28 days.

CHANGES FROM THE 1959 ACT

The Amendment Act changed the purpose of this category of compulsory admission from *observation* to *assessment* in order to clarify the fact that it can involve 'more active intervention to form a diagnosis and plan of treatment'.

The term *assessment,* in itself, may suggest that medical procedures must be limited to those which are necessary to form a diagnosis and to devise a plan of treatment, thus excluding procedures for the purpose of treatment (alleviating or curing the patient's condition). However, the bracketed phrase '(or for assessment followed by medical treatment)' suggests that active treatment *is* authorised, at least after an initial period of assessment. The fact that treatment is permitted under this section is confirmed by the inclusion of patients detained for assessment in the consent to treatment provisions of Part IV of the Act (see chapter 7). It may be, therefore, that – apart from the period of detention – there is very little difference between admission for assessment and admission for treatment.

In a new measure the 1983 Act gives patients admitted for assessment the right to apply to a Mental Health Review Tribunal within a period of 14 days following admission (s66(2)(a)). It also allows the nearest relative to discharge the patient, subject to certain provisions which give the responsible medical officer authority to bar the discharge. (For a wide-ranging discussion on all the provisions relating to discharge, see chapters 4 and 5.)

ADMISSION FOR TREATMENT

Statutory authority: s3

Maximum duration of detention: six months, renewable for a further six months and then for periods of one year at a time

Criteria: (a) the patient is suffering from mental illness, severe mental impairment, psychopathic disorder or mental impairment, and his mental disorder is of a nature or degree which makes it appropriate for him to receive medical treatment in a hospital; and

(b) in the case of psychopathic disorder or mental impairment, such treatment is likely to 'alleviate or prevent a deterioration of his condition'; and

(c) it is necessary for the health or safety of the patient or for the protection of others that he should receive such treatment and it cannot be provided unless he is detained under this section

Procedure: recommendation by two registered medical practitioners and an application by an approved social worker or the nearest relative

THE APPLICATION

An application for admission for treatment must be made by an approved social worker or the patient's nearest relative (s11(1)). However, an ASW cannot make an application under section 3 if the nearest relative has notified that social worker or the local authority social services department that he objects to the application being made. Even if no formal objection is raised, the approved social worker can only make an application after consulting the nearest relative *unless* this would not be 'reasonably practicable or would involve unreasonable delay' (s11(4)).

In sum, an approved social worker cannot make an application for admission for treatment until he has taken every practicable step to find out the views of the nearest relative, and he cannot make the application if the nearest relative objects. If a nearest relative raises unreasonable objections to an application being made, the only course of action open to the social worker is to ask the County Court to displace the nearest relative (see p 27).

The applicant must have personally seen the patient within a period of 14 days before the application is made (s11(5)). For the purposes of section 3, the application (and the two supporting medical recommendations) must specify the form of mental disorder. Both of the recommendations must specify the same form of disorder, although each of the medical practitioners is free to specify other forms as well. For example, if the application and the two medical recommendations all specify that the patient is suffering from psychopathic disorder, it does not matter if one or more also specifies mental illness.

MEDICAL RECOMMENDATIONS

An application for admission for treatment must be based on the written recommendations of two registered medical practitioners who state that criteria (a), (b) and (c) are satisfied. Each practitioner must give particular reasons for his opinion, and must state whether other methods of helping the patient are available and, if so, why they are not appropriate. One of the practitioners must be approved by the Secretary of State for Social Services as having special experience in the diagnosis or treatment of mental disorder (s12(2)).

Each of the doctors must give particulars in support of his opinion and confirm that no appropriate alternatives to hospital admission are available for the patient concerned. (For further requirements relating to medical recommendations, see p 17).

THE TREATABILITY REQUIREMENT

The Mental Health Act 1983 introduces the requirement that treatment must be 'likely to alleviate or prevent a deterioration of (the patient's) condition'. The treatability requirement applies only to the minor forms of mental disorder with the effect that a person classified as suffering from mental impairment or psychopathic disorder *cannot* be compulsorily admitted for treatment unless it is likely to alleviate or prevent a deterioration of his condition. There is no treatability requirement for the major forms of mental disorder (mental illness and severe mental impairment) at the time of admission; however, there is a *modified* treatability requirement which comes into force when the authority for detention is renewed. (See *Duration and renewal of detention,* p 14).

RECLASSIFICATION

If the responsible medical officer (RMO) feels that a patient admitted for treatment is suffering from a form of mental disorder other than that specified in the application, he can furnish the managers with a report stating that the patient is suffering from a different category of mental disorder. Should the medical officer reclassify the patient from a major to a minor disorder, he must indicate in his report to the managers whether the treatability requirement is fulfilled. If it is not, the authority for detention will cease. Before reclassifying a patient, the RMO must consult one or more people who have been professionally concerned with the patient's treatment, for example a nurse or social worker on the therapeutic team at the hospital (s16).

DURATION AND RENEWAL OF DETENTION

Patients admitted for treatment can be detained for a period of no longer than six months. The authority for detention can be renewed for a further six months and then for periods of one year at a time. To renew the authority for detention, the responsible medical officer must furnish a report to the managers stating that the original criteria for admission still apply. For the purposes of renewal, however, the treatability requirement is applied to all four forms of mental disorder, except that in the case of mental illness or severe mental impairment the 'untreatable' patient need not be discharged if he is 'unlikely to be able to care for himself, to obtain the care which he needs or to guard himself against serious exploitation' (s20(4)).

Thus, the authority to detain a person with a minor disorder can only be renewed if his condition is treatable; a renewal order can be made in respect of a person with a major disorder if his condition is treatable *or* if he is unable to obtain appropriate care or to guard himself against serious exploitation.

The RMO cannot furnish a report to renew the authority for detention unless he has examined the patient within a period of two months before the original detention order expires. He must also consult one or more people who have been professionally concerned with the patient's medical treatment (s20).

CHANGES FROM THE 1959 ACT

The primary change is the removal of the age limits which used to apply to the detention of people suffering from the minor disorders: these have been replaced by the new treatability requirement. It was felt that the age limits (21 in the case of admission; 25 in the case of patients already in hospital) were too inflexible. At the same time it was considered to be wrong to detain a patient suffering from a minor disorder unless there was a reasonable prospect that his condition was treatable.

The 1983 Act also reduces by half the periods for which patients compulsorily admitted for treatment can be detained. This means that a patient's case is subject to more frequent review, both by the RMO at the time the detention is renewed and by a Mental Health Review Tribunal.

Finally, the 1983 Act introduces the requirement that in specified circumstances the medical practitioner must consult other professionals who are involved in the care of the patient, a principle which underlines a number of provisions in the new Act. This requirement promotes good practice by making multidisciplinary consultation between members of the therapeutic team compulsory. In framing the 1983 Act, Parliament took the view that it was right in this instance to legislate for good practice.

RECEPTION INTO GUARDIANSHIP

Statutory authority: ss7-10

Maximum duration of detention: six months, renewable for a further six months and then for periods of one year at a time

Age limit: only a patient who has reached the age of 16 can be received into guardianship

Criteria: (a) the patient is suffering from mental illness, severe mental

impairment, psychopathic disorder or mental impairment, and his mental disorder is of a nature or degree which warrants his reception into guardianship; and
(b) it is necessary in the interests of the welfare of the patient or for the protection of others that the patient should be so received

Procedure: recommendation by two registered medical practitioners and an application by an approved social worker or the nearest relative. The guardian must be either a local social services authority or any person accepted by the authority for the area in which he (the guardian) lives

Effect: the guardian has the power to require the patient to live in a specified place and to attend specified places for the purpose of medical treatment, occupation, education or training. He can also require access to the patient to be given to any doctor, approved social worker or other specified person

THE APPLICATION

Only a patient who is aged 16 or older can be received into guardianship, and a guardianship application must be made by an approved social worker or the patient's nearest relative (s11(1)). The application must be addressed to the local social services authority for the area in which the guardian lives (s11(2)). As in the case of admission for treatment, an approved social worker cannot make an application for guardianship unless he has taken all reasonably practicable steps to consult the nearest relative, and no application can be made if the nearest relative objects (s11(4)). If the nearest relative raises unreasonable objections, or for other specified reasons, an approved social worker or other specified persons can apply to the County Court for an order appointing the ASW or any other proper person to act in place of the nearest relative (s30) (see p 27).

The applicant must have personally seen the patient within a period of 14 days before the application is made (s11(5)). The application must state the age of the patient or, if his exact age is not known, the fact that the patient is believed to have reached the age of 16 (s7(4)).

The guardian named in the application may either be a local social services authority or any other person (including the applicant himself). However, if the application names a person other than the local authority, this person must first be accepted as guardian by the authority for the area in which he lives. The person must also state in writing that he is willing to act as guardian.

MEDICAL RECOMMENDATIONS

A guardianship application must be based on the written recommendations of two registered medical practitioners stating that the relevant criteria are satisfied. Each practitioner must give particular reasons for his opinion, and one of them must be approved by the Secretary of State for Social Services as having special experience in the diagnosis or treatment of mental disorder (s12). Both medical practitioners must have examined the patient within a period of 14 days before the application is forwarded to the local social services authority (s8(2)).

EFFECT

Section 8 confers on the guardian a number of *specific* or *essential* powers namely—
  (i) to require the patient to reside at a place specified by the guardian;

(ii) to require the patient to attend at places and times specified for the purpose of medical treatment, occupation, education or training;

(iii) to require access to the patient to be given, at any place where the patient is residing, to any registered medical practitioner, approved social worker or other person specified by the guardian.

It may appear from point (ii) that a guardian can compel a patient to undergo a treatment to which he does not consent: this is, however, not the case. Guardianship patients enjoy the same common law rights as informal patients in respect of consent to treatment: this follows from the fact that guardianship patients are excluded from the consent to treatment provisions of Part IV of the Act because they are not 'liable to be detained'. Hence guardianship patients have the right to refuse any form of treatment.

When a patient is received into guardianship, any previous application for compulsory admission to hospital or reception into guardianship under Part II of the Act ceases to have effect (s8(5)).

Under the Mental Health Act 1983, there are specific penalties against a guardian who ill-treats or wilfully neglects a patient (s127(2)). It is also an offence to assist a guardianship patient to absent himself without leave (s128), or *without reasonable cause* to obstruct any authorised person from visiting, interviewing or examining a guardianship patient (s129). A local social services authority can institute proceedings in respect of any of these offences, subject to specific provisions requiring the consent of the Director of Public Prosecutions (s130).

REGULATIONS

The Secretary of State for Social Services is empowered to regulate the exercise of guardianship powers and to impose specific duties on guardians. In particular, regulations may require local authorities to arrange visits to patients on a regular basis. Regulations must also provide for the appointment of a doctor to act as the patient's nominated medical attendant in every case where guardianship is *not* undertaken by a local authority.

The Mental Health (Hospital and Guardianship and Consent to Treatment) Regulations 1983 have been issued in respect of the Mental Health Act 1983.

TRANSFER OF GUARDIANSHIP

Section 10 of the Act makes provision for guardianship of a patient to be transferred to the local social services authority in the event of his guardian's death or incapacity, or in cases where the guardian decides to relinquish his functions or the County Court finds that the guardian has exercised his functions negligently or in a manner contrary to the interests of the patient.

CHANGES FROM THE 1959 ACT

The age limits established by the 1959 Act in respect of the minor disorders no longer apply to guardianship patients. Children under the age of 16 cannot now be received into guardianship. Mentally disordered children who need care and control should therefore be dealt with under children's legislation or, if appropriate, through informal admission into hospital.

The 1959 Act conferred on a guardian all such powers as would be exercised by the father of a child under the age of 14. However, it was felt that these powers were too all-encompassing and tended to impose direct and far-reaching parental responsibilities upon the guardian. The Amendment Act 1982 therefore introduced a *specific* or *essential* powers approach. It also confirmed that guardianship patients could not be compelled to have treatment against their will.

These changes, which reduce the power of the guardian over the patient, were made primarily in order to encourage greater use of guardianship as a less restrictive alternative to hospital detention. It was envisaged that mentally impaired people in particular would benefit from greater use of more flexible guardianship provisions. The form of guardianship embodied in the 1983 Act should make it possible for many more patients to be cared for in the community without the need for compulsory admission to hospital. It is to be hoped that more local authorities will be prepared to receive patients into guardianship. However, authorities should not view guardianship simply as a way to excercise specified powers over a patient. Rather they should see it as a duty which imposes upon them a responsibility to provide appropriate help and support.

GENERAL REQUIREMENTS FOR MEDICAL RECOMMENDATIONS UNDER PART II OF THE ACT

The medical recommendations required for applications for compulsory admission under Part II of the Act must be signed on or before the date of the application by doctors who have personally examined the patient either together or within five days of each other (s12(1)).

Where two recommendations are required, one must be by a doctor approved under section 12 as having special experience in the diagnosis or treatment of mental disorder. If the approved doctor has not met the patient before, the other recommendation should — if practicable — be from a practitioner with previous knowledge of the patient.

Section 12(3) specifies that only one medical recommendation should be given by a doctor on the staff of the receiving hospital, unless compliance with this section would result in delay causing 'serious risk' to the patient or one of the doctors making a recommendation works for the hospital less than half time. The two recommendations cannot be given by doctors based at the same hospital if one of the practitioners concerned is a consultant and the other a doctor working under his direction (s12(4)). Furthermore, a doctor cannot make a recommendation if he is a close relative of the applicant or patient.

LEAVE OF ABSENCE

AUTHORISED LEAVE

The RMO can grant any patient detained under Part II of the Act leave of absence from the hospital, subject to such conditions, if any, as are considered necessary in the interests of the patient or the public. Indefinite leave may be granted, or a limited period may be specified. The RMO can recall a patient to hospital at any time during an authorised leave of absence by giving notice in writing to the patient or to the person temporarily in charge of him. However, in cases where the patient is on authorised leave of absence for a continuous period of six months, he is no longer subject to recall and ceases to be liable to be detained (s17). Furthermore, a patient on authorised leave cannot be detained beyond the expiration of the authority for his detention, even if six months have not elapsed.

Because a patient on authorised leave of absence is still 'liable to be detained', he is subject to the consent to treatment provisions of Part IV of the Act.

UNAUTHORISED LEAVE

A patient who is absent from hospital without the leave of the RMO can be taken into custody and returned to the hospital. However, a patient ceases to be liable to be detained and cannot be taken into custody after a period of 28 days continuous unauthorised absence from the hospital. Moreover, a patient cannot be taken into custody, even if 28 days have not elapsed, if the period for which he is liable to be detained for assessment, emergency assessment or the doctor's or nurse's holding power has expired. In certain circumstances if the patient returns to hospital before the period of detention expires, the authority for detention is extended by one week (s21).

It is not an offence for a patient to absent himself without leave, but a person who 'induces or knowingly assists' a patient to absent himself from hospital without authorisation, or who 'knowingly harbours' or provides assistance to such a person, *is* guilty of a criminal offence (s128).

MISCELLANEOUS PROVISIONS RELATING TO THE USE OF COMPULSION

Two sections in the 1983 Act give authority for compulsory detention, but require neither an application nor medical recommendations. They are therefore found not in Part II, which provides for compulsory admission to hospital and guardianship, but in Part X, which deals with miscellaneous provisions.

MENTALLY DISORDERED PERSONS FOUND IN PUBLIC PLACES

Statutory authority: s136

Maximum duration of detention: 72 hours

Criterion: it appears to a police officer that a person in a public place is 'suffering from mental disorder' and is 'in immediate need of care or control'

Procedure: *no* specific procedure required

Effect: person is taken to 'a place of safety' so that he can be examined by a medical practitioner and interviewed by an approved social worker, and 'any necessary arrangements' made for his treatment or care

If a police officer finds in a place to which the public have access a person who appears to be suffering from mental disorder and to be in immediate need of care or control, he may — if he thinks it necessary in the person's interest or for the protection of others — remove that person to a place of safety. A person thus removed to a place of safety may be detained for a period of up to 72 hours in order that he can be examined by a registered medical practitioner and interviewed by an approved social worker, and any necessary arrangements made for his treatment or care.

This section of the 1959 Act was left unamended by the 1982 Act although it has been the subject of extensive criticism. This criticism is centred primarily on the fact that the section gives individual police officers considerable scope to use their own discretion, as is illustrated by the wide regional variation in the use of the power. Concern has also been expressed that police officers do not have adequate training or experience in the identification of mental disorder, and that removal to 'a place of safety' often means to a police station. In view of the degree of concern, it is worth examining the terms of this provision in greater detail.

A place to which the public have access: this would include a park, railway station etc, but not a person's home. In *Carter* v *Commissioner of Police of the Metropolis [1975] 1 WLR 507, 513,* a woman was taken to a place of safety following a quarrel on the front step of her home. She claimed that she was not mentally disordered and had therefore been falsely imprisoned, but the High Court refused to grant her permission under section 139 (previously section 141 of the 1959 Act) to bring an action in court against the police officer. It could have been successfully argued in this case that the woman concerned was not in a *public place.*

. . . appears to be suffering from mental disorder: this phrase indicates that the person need not actually be mentally disordered; the police officer must only have a reasonable belief that this is the case. A police officer acting in good faith and with reasonable care has the protection of section 139 (see pp 61-63).

Place of safety: this means residential accommodation provided by the social services department, a hospital, a police station or any other suitable place which is willing to receive the patient (s135(6)). A residential home or hospital is not obliged to admit patients brought in by the police under section 136, and some are reluctant to do so. The DHSS has advised that a police station should only be used in exceptional circumstances. If a police station *is* used, the patient should remain there for no longer than a few hours while an approved social worker makes the necessary arrangements for removal elsewhere, either informally or under Part II of the Act.

Purpose and duration of detention: section 136 is designed to provide an opportunity for the patient to be examined by a doctor and interviewed by an approved social worker, and for any necessary arrangements to be made for his treatment or care. A person cannot simply be detained in custody without arrangements being made for the appropriate interviews and examinations. Moreover, once these interviews have been completed the authority for detention lapses, even if 72 hours have not yet expired.

WARRANT TO SEARCH FOR AND REMOVE PATIENTS

Statutory authority: s135
Maximum duration of detention: 72 hours
Criterion: there is 'reasonable cause to suspect that a person believed to be suffering from mental disorder' has been (a) ill-treated or neglected or not kept under proper control, or is (b) unable to care for himself and is living alone
Procedure: an approved social worker lays information on oath before a Justice of the Peace
Effect: a constable (accompanied by a doctor and an approved social worker) can enter the patient's premises and remove him to a place of safety

Any approved social worker who has reasonable cause to believe that a person is suffering from a mental disorder and (a) 'has been, or is being, ill-treated, neglected or kept otherwise than under proper control', or (b) is living alone and is unable to care for himself, can apply to a Justice of the Peace for a warrant. The warrant authorises a police officer, accompanied by an approved social worker and registered doctor, to enter the person's premises, if necessary by force, and – if appropriate – to remove him to a place of safety (defined on p 19) for a period of up to 72 hours.

CHAPTER 3

THE ROLE OF THE APPROVED SOCIAL WORKER & THE NEAREST RELATIVE

THE ROLE OF THE APPROVED SOCIAL WORKER

The powers and duties of social workers and social services departments were significantly changed by the Amendment Act, and it is therefore useful to examine the role of the social worker in some detail. In the 1983 Act the term *local social services authority* indicates a council which is a local authority for the purposes of the Local Authority Social Services Act 1970 (s145(1)). Local authorities are the councils of non-metropolitan counties, metropolitan districts and London boroughs, and the Common Council of the City of London.

APPOINTMENT OF APPROVED SOCIAL WORKERS

The Amendment Act acknowledged that social workers exercising powers conferred by the Mental Health Act — currently called mental welfare officers (MWOs) — need appropriate training and experience. Accordingly, two years after the passage of the Amendment Act (ie 28 October 1984) the duties conferred on MWOs will become the responsibility of *approved social workers* (ASWs). Social services authorities will have a statutory obligation to appoint 'a sufficient number of approved social workers for the purpose of discharging the functions conferred on them by this Act' (s114(1)). No person can be appointed as an ASW unless he is approved by the department as 'having appropriate competence in dealing with persons who are suffering from mental disorder' (s114(2)). In approving a person, departments must 'have regard to such matters as the Secretary of State may direct' (s114(3)), and directions on the appointment of ASWs are issued by the Department of Health and Social Security (DHSS). (See local authority circular 83/7).

The approval of social workers is a matter solely for local authorities who are also responsible for developing training programmes. However, local authorities cannot approve a social worker unless he has first passed the examination set by the Central Council for Education and Training in Social Work (CCETSW). Social workers submitting themselves for approval must show that they have knowledge of the legislation relevant to the powers and duties of ASWs; knowledge of the nature of mental disorder within family, social and cultural contexts and of available treatments; and knowledge of appropriate local and national provision and its use in the care and support of clients and their families (CCETSW, *Regulations for the assessment of social workers who are to be considered for approval under mental health legislation* (July 1983)).

THE DUTY TO MAKE APPLICATIONS FOR ADMISSION OR GUARDIANSHIP

The Mental Health Act places on an ASW the duty to make an application for admission to hospital or reception into guardianship in respect of any patient within the area of the local social services authority by whom he is appointed, *if* he is satisfied that such an application should be made. In forming his opinion, the ASW must take account of any wishes expressed by the patient's relatives and any other relevant circumstances (s13(1)).

Section 13 does not oblige the social worker to make an application if, in his professional judgement, it is not necessary for an application to be made. Although he is required to take into account the views of relatives and any other relevant circumstances, probably including medical opinion, he should not be pressured into making an application which he considers unnecessary simply because his view differs from that of the doctor or relative. On the contrary, the ASW should make an application *only* if he is completely satisfied that the statutory criteria are fulfilled (s13(5)).

An ASW *may* make an application outside the area of the social services department by whom he is appointed, but there is no statutory obligation for him to do so (s13(3)). This might be necessary, for example, where two social services authorities share an 'out of house' service, or where a patient is admitted informally to a hospital outside his authority and then has to be compulsorily detained.

The liberty interest

The statutory functions of the ASW relate primarily (but not exclusively) to matters which affect the liberty of the individual. Parliament expressly decided that there should be an application based upon particular statutory criteria (s13(2)) which would be separate from the supporting medical recommendations. The ASW's powers and duties under section 13 would not have been enacted if it had been intended that medical opinion alone should authorise compulsory admission. Each professional should be expected to contribute to the final decision only what is appropriate to his own knowledge and experience. Mental health legislation has for some time recognised that mental disorder alone does not render a person liable to be detained; the person's social situation and community-based alternatives to hospital care must also be taken into account. Assessment of these latter factors is the ASW's primary claim to a professional as distinct from a purely procedural role. The ASW therefore has a responsibility to maintain complete independence and impartiality when assessing a patient's needs in the context of his family and social situation, and the care and support which can, and *should*, be provided in the community.

In each case of compulsory admission, whether it be for benevolent reasons or for the prevention of physical harm to others, a person is deprived of liberty. The statutory procedure for admission must be followed strictly and accurately, and it is the responsibility of the ASW to see that this is so, both in his capacity as a statutory officer with duties conferred by the Act and as a professional seeking to ensure that care and treatment are provided in the least restrictive setting possible. The protection of a patient's 'liberty interest' is particularly important because compulsory admission under Part II of the Act does not require prior judicial review.

HOSPITAL-BASED SOCIAL WORKERS

There are sometimes uncertainties as to whether a hospital-based social worker should make an application for compulsory admission. It can be argued that there are insufficient safeguards for the patient when the social worker making the application is an integral part of the multidisciplinary therapeutic team in the receiving hospital. The hospital-based social worker may also have too little opportunity to provide effective support for the family in the community and to investigate community care provision in great enough detail. Some social services departments consider it good practice to prohibit hospital-based social workers from making applications. Others, however, believe that hospital-based social workers have the greatest mental health expertise and *should* be permitted to make applications. Such departments also point out that in rural communities there may be a very limited number of approved social workers so that it may be essential to use those who are based in hospitals.

MIND has always tended towards the view that, wherever possible, applications should be made by ASWs who are not associated with the receiving hospital, thus ensuring independence of opinion. Nonetheless, there is nothing in the Mental Health Act to preclude applications from hospital-based social workers, and such applications appear to be lawful.

CHANGES FROM THE 1959 ACT

The Mental Health Act 1983 charges social services authorities and ASWs with three new responsibilities: the duty to interview; the duty to direct an approved social worker to consider making an application; and the duty to prepare a social report.

The duty to interview

Before making an application for admission the ASW must
> 'interview the patient in a suitable manner and satisfy himself that detention in a hospital is in all the circumstances of the case the most appropriate way of providing the care and medical treatment of which the patient stands in need' (s13(2)).

Thus, before completing an application for admission to hospital, the ASW must interview the patient *in a suitable manner,* which means he must speak with the patient *in person* in order to find out the relevant information. It is insufficient for him to accept information from an indirect or second-hand source, for example a doctor, without speaking to the patient face-to-face. In a case brought by MIND which was determined before the Act was passed, but which influenced the Bill during its passage through Parliament (Complaint No INV 411/H/80 against Isle of Wight County Council 8/9/81), the Local Government Commissioner held that a social worker acted improperly in signing an appllication without first ensuring that all the statutory requirements had been fulfilled. The social worker concerned *had* interviewed the patient, but had not taken steps to satisfy himself that the general practitioner who signed the recommendation had also done so.

The ASW must also conduct the interview 'in a suitable manner'. This phrase is not defined in detail, but probably means that, wherever possible, the interview must be conducted at a level which is comprehensible to the patient, taking into account any difficulties the patient may have with the English language or with his hearing. The conduct of an interview in which the patient refuses to co-operate, or is unable or unwilling to articulate his views, may be quite different from that of one where the patient is able and willing to supply relevant information on his social circumstances.

If a patient locks himself in his room and a personal interview is impossible, it may be argued that talking (without response) through the door is an interview *in a suitable manner.* However, the more likely view is that no interview can take place in these circumstances, and therefore no application can be made. In such cases, if no-one who knows the patient can persuade him to come out of his room, it may be necessary for the ASW to ask a Justice of the Peace for a warrant to search for and remove him (s135) (see pp 19-20).

Following the interview, the ASW must satisfy himself that 'in all the circumstances of the case' hospital admission is 'the most appropriate way' of providing the care and treatment the patient needs (s13(2)). From the patient's perspective, the *most* appropriate form of treatment is likely to be provided in the setting which makes the least restrictions on his liberty as an individual. Thus, if treatment and care can be provided as, or more, effectively in a community environment, this is preferable to compulsory admission. The social worker should examine the patient's personal, social and family circumstances, and should investigate whether there are any support systems other than a hospital which could provide the appropriate care and treatment. He should determine how much social support can be given to the patient and his family, preferably in their own community.

Medical diagnosis is not the responsibility of the ASW, although he must take account of the doctor's opinion, and must be aware of the significance of a person's feelings, behaviour and social environment.

The duty to direct an approved social worker to consider making an application

It is the duty of a local social services authority – if so requested by the nearest relative of a patient living in its area – to direct an ASW, as soon as practicable, to consider whether an application for compulsory admission should be made (s13(4)). This does not mean that the ASW is required to make an application, only that he must exercise his professional judgement (s13(5)). It might well mean that the social worker *is* required to take steps to interview the patient, although this is not expressly stated in the Act. If the ASW decides *not* to make an application, he must inform the nearest relative of his reasons in writing.

Social reports

Except in the case of emergency admission (s4), when a patient is admitted to hospital under Part II of the Act through an application made by the nearest relative, the hospital managers must, as soon as practicable, notify the local social services authority for the area where the patient lived immediately before his admission. The authority must then, as soon as practicable, arrange for a social worker from the social services department to interview the patient and to provide the hospital managers with a report on his social circumstances (s14). It would have been preferable had Parliament required that a social report be prepared *before* rather than *after* admission. Nonetheless, this provision does establish the importance of having a full social report in every case of compulsory detention (except admissions under section 4).

It is significant that the social services authority can direct any of its social workers to interview the patient; it need *not* be an approved social worker. This was an intentional decision reflecting the view that the social worker concerned should be a person who is available to, and works with, the patient's family. It emphasises the importance of having a social worker with a continuing responsibility for the patient and his family.

The provision means that social services departments are not obliged to use ASWs to prepare social reports, although it does not of course preclude the use of ASWs in this capacity.

After-care reports for tribunals

When a patient who is liable to be detained applies to a MHRT, the hospital managers are required to prepare a social circumstances report on him (MHRT Rules 1983, SI 1983 no 942, rule 6). The responsible social services authority has the same duty in respect of a guardianship patient appearing before a tribunal. In practice these reports are always prepared on behalf of the social services authority, although not necessarily by an approved social worker. Such reports have sometimes been incomplete in the past because the social worker concerned felt that the patient did not have a realistic chance of being discharged by the tribunal. However, this is an unlawful consideration since it prejudges the tribunal's decision, and indeed prejudices the patient's chance of being discharged.

Perhaps the most important information required by the members of the MHRT concerns arrangements for the patient's after-care. Rule 6 and schedule 1 of the MHRT Rules of Procedure stipulate that the social circumstances report must include full information about the patient's home situation (including financial circumstances and family history); employment and housing prospects in the area where the patient would live if he were discharged; the attitude of the nearest relative; and the availability of medical facilities (including out-patient provision) and community support.

This information should be regarded as the *minimum* requirement: in each individual case the social worker preparing the report should present the MHRT with *all* relevant details on the patient's social circumstances and after-care arrangements. Moreover, the patient's representative and/or the MHRT itself may ask an officer of the social services authority to attend the hearing in order to give oral evidence. The patient's representative can also commission an independent social enquiry report, the costs of which can often be met from the legal aid fund.

IMPLICATIONS FOR SOCIAL WORK PRACTICE

The 1959 Act did not specify minimum levels of competence, experience or training for MWOs. Practice among local authorities varied widely: some warranted most or all social work staff as MWOs; others also warranted unqualified and untrained staff with minimal experience in mental health.

The Mental Health Act 1983, and accompanying directions issued by the Secretary of State (LAC/83/7), require that local authorities should only approve social workers with sufficient training and experience to demonstrate 'appropriate competence in dealing with persons who are suffering from mental disorder' (s114(2)). The general objective is to improve and maintain the quality and standards of social work practice in mental health. The demonstrated competence of ASWs should not be limited to specific responsibilities (eg in relation to applications for compulsory admission) conferred on them by the Mental Health Act, important as these are. It would be wrong for the role of the ASW to be relegated to that of a statutory officer exercising a purely administrative/legal responsibility. Rather, the ASW should be concerned with all the aspects of professional social work practice necessarily implied by his statutory obligations: the personal interview (requiring sensitive communication with the patient and his family); the investigation of the least restrictive treatment and care settings (requiring a detailed knowledge of services provided by the local authority and voluntary organisations); and the prevention, wherever possible, of the use of compulsory admission through crisis intervention and management, as well as support for the patient and his family.

When hospitalisation is found to be the most appropriate way of providing the necessary treatment and care, the ASW's involvement should not end after an application for compulsory admission has been completed. The ASW should sustain the relationship with the patient and his family after the admission in order to pave the way for the patient's return to a normal community environment. However, the principle of avoiding admission to hospital wherever possible, and of returning hospitalised patients to the community, should become the focus of the social worker's role under the 1983 Act.

FUNCTIONS OF RELATIVES

DETERMINING THE NEAREST RELATIVE

For the purposes of Part II of the Act, the term *relative* means any of the following (s26(I))—

(a)   husband or wife;
(b)   son or daughter;
(c)   father or mother;
(d)   brother or sister;
(e)   grandparent;
(f)   grandchild;
(g)   uncle or aunt;
(h)   nephew or niece.

The *nearest* relative is the 'person first described'. If a patient has two relatives of the same standing (for example father *and* mother), the elder is considered to be the nearest relative; the nearest relative is not determined by gender (s26(3)). If a patient 'ordinarily resides with or is cared for by' one or more of his relatives (or resided with or was cared for by them immediately before he was admitted to hospital), those relatives are given preference over all others (s26(4)).

There is a number of detailed criteria to determine accurately who the nearest relative is (s26): the patient's preference is not taken into account. Included in these criteria is the provision that a person who is, or was immediately before the admission, living with the patient *as husband or wife,* and had done so for a period of six months or more, is treated as the patient's spouse. This provision only applies to married patients if they are permanently separated (s26(5)(b)). A person who is not a relative and is not living with the patient as husband or wife, but who *has* lived with the patient for five years or more, is considered to be a relative (although not necessarily the nearest relative) (s26(7)). However the person who has lived with the patient for at least five years would take precedence over all other relatives who are not residing with or caring for the patient. In such circumstances *that* person would be the nearest relative. This provision resulted from an amendment to the Mental Health (Amendment) Bill which was designed to cover non-relatives of the same sex who live together.

In sum, if a patient lives (or, immediately before his admission, lived) with a *relative,* that person is the nearest relative; if he has lived with a *non-relative as husband or wife* for six months, that person is the nearest relative; if he has lived with a *non-relative but not as husband and wife* for five years, that person is in law a relative, but not necessarily the nearest relative.

The lawful guardian of a patient under the age of 18 is considered to be the nearest relative (s28). In cases where 'the rights and powers of a parent of a patient' are vested in a local authority or another person by virtue of sections 3 or 10 of the Child Care Act 1980, that authority or person is considered to be the nearest relative (s27).

APPOINTMENT BY COURT OF ACTING NEAREST RELATIVE

A County Court has the power to direct that the functions of the nearest relative be exercised by another authority or person. An application to the County Court for a displacement order can be made by *any* relative of the patient, by any person with whom he lives (or lived before his admission), or by an approved social worker. The grounds for such an application would be that the patient has no nearest relative, or that the nearest relative is incompetent, objects unreasonably to an application for admission or has exercised his power of discharge without due regard to the interests of the patient or the public.

The court can make an order directing that the functions of the nearest relative should be exercised by the applicant, or by a person specified in the application who is willing to act as nearest relative and is considered to be a 'proper person' to do so (s29).

A displacement order may be discharged or varied upon application to the County Court (s30), and there are County Court rules setting out the procedures for applications (s31).

POWERS OF NEAREST RELATIVE

The Act gives *nearest* relatives a number of powers: in particular, they have the right to make an application for compulsory admission to hospital or guardianship under Part II (s11(1)); the right to exercise a discharge order in respect of patients admitted for assessment or treatment (s23(2)); and the power to require an approved social worker to consider making an application for admission under Part II (s13(4)). Very few specific functions are conferred on relatives who are not the nearest relative, but the views of any relative must be taken into account before an application for admission is made by an ASW (s13(1)).

CHAPTER 4

DISCHARGE FROM HOSPITAL & GUARDIANSHIP

The Mental Health Act gives the right to discharge a detained patient to the responsible medical officer (RMO), the managers, the nearest relative or a Mental Health Review Tribunal (MHRT). The precise means of discharge is determined by the section under which the patient is detained. When a discharge is considered, the primary concern must always be with the justification for the patient's continued detention; the lawfulness of the initial admission is not at issue. If there is reason to believe that the initial admission was unlawful (for example if the necessary applications and recommendations were not completed properly), the patient has recourse to judicial remedies such as the writ of *habeas corpus.*

The forms ot discharge described in this chapter are, strictly speaking, only applicable to patients detained under Part II (and, by reference, to unrestricted patients detained under Part III). However, it is almost certain that either the RMO or the managers could discharge a patient admitted by a police officer or by a Justice's warrant. In any case, the authority for detention in these categories of admission ceases after the necessary interviews and examinations have been completed (see pp 18-20).

DISCHARGE BY THE RMO OR MANAGERS

A patient who is detained in *hospital* for treatment or assessment can be discharged by the RMO or the hospital managers (s23(2)(a)). A patient detained for assessment or treatment in a *mental nursing home* can be discharged by the RMO or the managers; he can also be discharged by the Secretary of State for Social Services (s23(3)). Either the RMO or the responsible social services department can discharge a patient from guardianship.

The powers of discharge conferred on the managers can be exercised by any three or more members of the District Health Authority (s23(4)).

The right of the RMO or the managers to discharge a detained patient is not subject to any statutory criteria and can be exercised at any time during the applicable period of detention.

DISCHARGE BY THE NEAREST RELATIVE

The nearest relative has the power to order the discharge of a patient who is detained for treatment or for assessment (unless this is the result of an emergency application), or who is subject to guardianship (s23(2)). In the case of a patient detained for treatment or assessment, the nearest relative must give the managers a minimum of 72 hours notice in writing of his intention to discharge the patient. Within that 72 hour period the RMO can furnish the managers with a report certifying that, in his opinion, the patient 'would be likely to act in a manner dangerous to other persons or to himself' if discharged, and the discharge order is then void. No further order can be made for a period of six months (s25). If the RMO furnishes a report barring the patient's discharge in the case of a person admitted for treatment, the nearest relative can, within the following 28 days, apply to a MHRT requesting the patient's discharge (s66).

In the case of a patient subject to guardianship, there is no requirement for 72 hours notice to be given. The nearest relative's discharge order cannot be barred by the RMO or any other person.

DISCHARGE BY A MENTAL HEALTH REVIEW TRIBUNAL

Mental Health Review Tribunals have the power to discharge certain patients who are subject to detention or guardianship under Part II of the Act. Patients under the age of 16 can now apply to a MHRT for the first time. A full description of the composition, procedures and powers of MHRTs is given in chapter 6.

AUTOMATIC REFERENCE

The Mental Health Act 1959 was open to the criticism that it placed the burden of applying to a MHRT on the patient or nearest relative; less than 20 per cent of those eligible to apply actually exercised their right to do so. In response to this concern, the 1983 Act imposes on hospital managers the duty to refer to a tribunal any patient detained for treatment who has not had a tribunal hearing in the first six months of his detention. The managers are also required to refer to a MHRT any patient who has been detained for three years (one year in the case of children under 16) without a tribunal hearing (s68).

These provisions ensure that patients who lack the ability or initiative to make an application to a tribunal will have the safeguard of an independent review of their case. As in the 1959 Act, the Secretary of State for Social Services still has the right to refer cases to a tribunal, but this is a *discretionary* power and not a duty (s67).

CHAPTER 5

PATIENTS CONCERNED IN CRIMINAL PROCEEDINGS

Traditionally, mentally disordered offenders were exempted from punishment if they were not considered responsible for their acts *(not guilty by reason of insanity)*, or if they were unable to understand the proceedings of the trial *(unfit to stand trial)*. To gain such an exemption, it was necessary to demonstrate a causal relationship between the person's mental disorder and either the commission of the crime, or the defendant's ability to understand and participate in the trial. The defence of *not guilty by reason of insanity* and the plea of *unfitness to stand trial* are still available, but they are difficult to sustain and are very rarely used today. When they *are* successful, the judge is *required* by law to make an order under the Criminal Procedure (Insanity) Act 1964 which has the same effect as a hospital order with restrictions on discharge without limit of time.

Since the Mental Health Act 1959 was enacted, the use of the hospital order (with or without restrictions on discharge) has virtually replaced that of the insanity defence (sometimes called the *special verdict*) and the plea of unfitness to stand trial (sometimes called *disability in relation to the trial*). In making a hospital order the judge is not concerned with criminal responsibility or causality; indeed the person concerned has usually been tried and convicted already. The judge only has to consider the most appropriate means of dealing with the offender – ie he must determine whether the person is mentally disordered and in need of treatment.

Broadly speaking, there are three points at which a person can be sent to hospital: at the time of his trial he can be *remanded to hospital;* at the time of sentencing he can be given an *interim hospital order*, a *hospital order* (with or without restrictions) or a *guardianship order;* after he has been sentenced to a term of imprisonment he can be *transferred* to hospital. Each of these possibilities is described in this chapter.

There is also a number of other ways in which an offender's mental condition may be placed at issue, although these will not be discussed in detail. A person charged with murder can plead *diminished responsibility,* ie that he was suffering from such 'abnormality of mind as substantially impaired his responsibility in being a party to the killing'. A conviction of murder carries a fixed sentence of life imprisonment, and a hospital order cannot be made. However, a successful plea of diminished responsibility reduces the charge from murder to manslaughter, thus giving the judge discretion to make a hospital order if he thinks appropriate.

At the time of sentencing, the judge can opt to make a *probation order with a condition of psychiatric treatment.* This is like any other probation order, and means that the offender can remain in the community while receiving the treatment he needs. He may enter hospital as an informal patient, or he may be treated on an out-patient basis. A person on a psychiatric probation order cannot be given treatment against his will.

REMANDS TO HOSPITAL

The Mental Health Act 1983 adopts proposals originally put forward by the Butler Committee for remand to hospital for a medical report; remand to hospital for treatment; and an interim hospital order to determine whether a hospital order would be suitable. The object of these proposals is to provide an opportunity for a person who has been brought before a court to be examined or treated in hospital for a limited period before the court takes a final decision in his case. Because the proposals have significant resource implications for the NHS, they will not be implemented until a date to be specified by the Secretary of State (s149); it is expected that they will be implemented, in stages if necessary, within two or three years of the passage of the Amendment Act 1982.

REMAND FOR REPORT

Statutory authority: s35

Maximum duration of detention: 28 days. with further periods of 28 days for not more than 12 weeks in all

Criteria: (a) there is 'reason to suspect' that the accused person is suffering from mental illness, psychopathic disorder, severe mental impairment or mental impairment; and
(b) it would be 'impracticable' for a report on his mental condition to be made if he were remanded on bail

Procedure: remand by a Crown Court or Magistrates' Court on the evidence of a medical practitioner

A Crown Court or Magistrates' Court can remand an accused person to hospital for a report on his medical condition if satisfied, on the written or oral evidence of a registered medical practitioner, that criteria (a) and (b) are fulfilled. The practitioner must be one approved by the Secretary of State for Social Services under section 12 'as having special experience in the diagnosis or treatment of mental disorder' (s54(1)). The court cannot remand a person for report unless satisfied, on the written or oral evidence of the doctor who would be responsible for making the report or some other person representing the hospital managers, that arrangements have been made for the patient's admission to hospital within a period of seven days after the remand order is made.

The provisions of section 35 should only be used if it is inappropriate to remand the person on bail; in cases where bail is justified, it may be possible to obtain a medical report if the accused person is prepared to be examined by a psychiatrist on an in-patient or out-patient basis.

The court can further remand the accused person in his absence (as long as he is represented) if it is satisfied, on the evidence of the doctor responsible for preparing the report, that a further remand is necessary in order to complete the psychiatric assessment. An accused person cannot be remanded or further remanded for more than 28 days at a time, or for more than 12 weeks in total.

A person remanded for report is entitled to commission an independent psychiatric report at his own expense, and to apply to the court for his remand to be terminated. He is not subject to the consent to treatment provisions of Part IV of the Act, and therefore retains his common law right to refuse treatment.

REMAND FOR TREATMENT

Statutory authority: s36

Maximum duration of detention: 28 days, with further periods of 28 days for not more than 12 weeks in all

Criterion: the accused person is suffering from mental illness or severe mental impairment 'of a nature or degree which makes it appropriate for him to be detained in a hospital for medical treatment'

Procedure: remand by a Crown Court on the evidence of two medical practitioners

Rather than remanding an accused person in custody, a Crown Court has the power to remand him to hospital for treatment if satisfied, on the evidence of two registered medical practitioners (one of whom is approved under section 12), that the relevant criterion is fulfilled. Only patients classified as suffering from a major form of mental disorder can be remanded for treatment, but otherwise the provisions of section 36 are similar to those of section 35 (remand for report): evidence from the RMO or hospital managers is required to show that arrangements have been made for the patient's admission to hospital; the court has the power to remand or further remand him for 28 days at a time for a total of not more than 12 weeks in all; the accused person can commission an independent medical report at his own expense. In contrast to section 35, however, a person remanded for treatment *is* subject to the consent to treatment provisions of Part IV of the Act.

Mental condition of those accused of murder

Because the sentence is fixed by law, a person accused of murder cannot be remanded for treatment under section 36. This is regrettable because a person accused of this crime may be severely mentally ill or handicapped, and in urgent need of treatment or appropriate training. However, section 34 of the Mental Health (Amendment) Act 1982 amends the Bail Act 1976 so that, in the case of a person accused of murder, a court can impose as a condition of bail the requirement that (i) the person is examined by two doctors who will prepare medical reports on him; and (ii) he attends an institution or place as directed by the court for the purpose of having these reports prepared.

HOSPITAL ORDER

Statutory authority: s37

Maximum duration of detention: six months, renewable for a further six months and then for periods of one year at a time

Criteria: (a) the offender is suffering from mental illness, psychopathic disorder, severe mental impairment or mental impairment of a nature or degree which makes it appropriate for him to be detained for medical treatment; and
(b) in the case of psychopathic disorder or mental impairment, such treatment 'is likely to alleviate or prevent a deterioration of his condition'; and
(c) the court is of the opinion, 'having regard to all the circumstances including the nature of the offence and the character and antecedents of the offender, and to the

other available methods of dealing with him', that the most suitable method of disposing of the case is by means of a hospital order

Procedure: order by Crown Court or Magistrates' Court on the evidence of two medical practitioners

CROWN COURT: An offence punishable with imprisonment

A Crown Court can make a hospital order in the case of a person convicted of an offence punishable with imprisonment. It *cannot* make a hospital order if the crime concerned is murder as the sentence (life imprisonment) is mandatory, but can do so in the case of a person convicted of manslaughter with diminished responsibility. This is why solicitors very often submit a plea of diminished responsibility in cases where the accused person is charged with murder. If this plea is accepted, a person who has committed homicide will be convicted of manslaughter and a hospital order can then be made, if appropriate.

MAGISTRATES' COURT: A hospital order without recording a conviction

A Magistrates' Court can make a hospital or guardianship order in the case of a person convicted of an offence punishable *on summary conviction* with imprisonment. It can also make a hospital order *without* recording a conviction if the person is classified as suffering from mental illness or severe mental impairment, and the court is satisfied that he did commit the act with which he is charged. This discretion is exercised in cases where it would be inappropriate to convict a person charged with a relatively minor offence and where a conviction would prove stigmatising. When a magistrate makes a hospital or guardianship order without recording a conviction, the person is still entitled to appeal against the order as if it had been made on conviction (s45).

CRITERIA

The court must be satisfied, on the written or oral evidence of two registered medical practitioners, that the criteria (a), (b) and (c) are fulfilled. These criteria incorporate the *treatability requirement* which also applies to admission for treatment (see p 13). *A modified treatability requirment* comes into force when a hospital order is renewed, as for patients detained under Part II (see p 14).

ARRANGEMENTS FOR ADMISSION TO HOSPITAL

A hospital order cannot be made unless a court is satisfied, on the written or oral evidence of the doctor who would be in charge of treatment or another person representing the managers, that arrangements have been made for the patient's admission to hospital within a period of 28 days. This provision gives the receiving hospital considerable leeway to decide whether or not to accept a patient and, as a result, courts have sometimes experienced difficulty in finding a hospital willing to accommodate a mentally disordered offender. The Act therefore empowers courts to require representatives from the appropriate Regional Health Authority to provide information about potential receiving hospitals. (See *Information for the court* on p 35).

THE EFFECT OF A HOSPITAL ORDER AND THE METHOD OF DISCHARGE

The effect of a hospital order is similar to that of admission for treatment under Part II of the Act, ie the patient is detained for a period of up to six months, renewable for a further six months and then for periods of one year at a time (s40). As in the case of admission for treatment, the patient can be discharged by the RMO, the hospital managers or a MHRT. However, a patient on a hospital order cannot be discharged by his nearest relative: instead the nearest relative has the right to apply to a MHRT within the period between six and twelve months after the date of the hospital order, and in any subsequent period of twelve months. The patient himself is not entitled to apply to a tribunal within the first six months of admission; the periods when he *is* eligible to apply are the same as those for the nearest relative.

A hospital order can be made with or without restrictions on discharge (see pp 36-38).

CHANGES FROM THE 1959 ACT

Most of the Amendment Act provisions which relate to civil admissions also apply in the case of offender-patients. The criteria for making a hospital order have been changed in line with the reformed civil admission for treatment: *mental impairment* has replaced the term *subnormality*, and the courts cannot make a hospital order in respect of a person suffering from a minor disorder unless the *treatability* criterion is satisfied. Hospital order patients also benefit from shorter periods of detention and more frequent access to MHRTs, plus the *treatability* or *modified treatability* requirements which come into force when the hospital order is renewed.

Under the 1959 Act, a hospital order patient had the right to apply to a MHRT within his first six months of admission, but this right was removed in order to make the legal position of hospital order patients consistent with that of restricted patients who have never had the right to apply to a MHRT in the first six months of detention. The Government felt that this consistency was required by the European Convention on Human Rights, although MIND is of the opinion that the Convention would not require the diminishing of a patient's rights in this way.

GUARDIANSHIP

Statutory authority: s37
Maximum duration of detention: as for a hospital order
Criteria: as for a hospital order except that an offender must be aged 16 or older and suffering from a mental disorder 'of a nature or degree which warrants his reception into guardianship'
Procedure: as for a hospital order

The criteria, procedure and maximum duration of detention in respect of guardianship orders made by the courts are virtually identical to those which relate to hospital orders. However, a court can only make a guardianship order in the case of an offender who has reached the age of 16.

The effect of a guardianship order made by a court is the same as that of a guardianship application under Part II of the Act (s40) (see pp 14-17).

INTERIM HOSPITAL ORDER

Statutory authority: s38

Maximum duration of detention: 12 weeks, renewable for 28 days at a time but for no more than six months in all

Criteria: (a) the offender is suffering from mental illness, psychopathic disorder, severe mental impairment or mental impairment; and
(b) there is reason to suppose that the mental disorder 'is such that it may be appropriate for a hospital order to be made'

Procedure: order by a Crown Court or Magistrates' Court on the evidence of two medical practitioners

When a person is convicted before a Crown Court or Magistrates' Court and the court is satisfied, on the evidence of two medical practitioners, that the relevant criteria are fulfilled, it can make an interim hospital order. The court must also be satisfied, on the evidence of the RMO or another representative of the managers, that arrangements have been made for the patient's admission to hospital within 28 days.

An interim hospital order remains in force for a period which is specified by the court but which cannot exceed 12 weeks. It can be renewed for further periods of 28 days at a time after the court has heard evidence from the RMO, but an interim hospital order cannot continue in force for more than six months in total.

The court can renew an interim order or make a full hospital order in the case of a patient already in hospital on an interim hospital order in the absence of the patient himself, *provided* his counsel or solicitor is given the opportunity of being heard.

A patient on an interim hospital order is subject to the consent to treatment provisions in Part IV of the Act. There is a civil liberties concern about the use of interim hospital orders. Consider the case of a court which, after making an interim order for up to six months, decides to pass a sentence of imprisonment. The time spent in hospital is not discounted from the total prison sentence even though the person lost his liberty while in hospital.

INFORMATION FOR THE COURT

A court which is considering making a hospital order or an interim hospital order can ask the Regional Health Authority (or the Secretary of State for Wales) to provide it with information about hospitals where arrangements might be made for the patient's admission (s39). This provision was introduced in the Mental Health (Amendment) Act 1982 in order to help courts to find hospitals which are willing to admit mentally disordered offenders. It is intended to help the courts avoid sentencing a seriously mentally disordered person to prison by requiring the RHA to explain why a hospital bed cannot be found.

REQUIREMENTS RELATING TO MEDICAL EVIDENCE

Part III of the Act generally stipulates that when only one medical recommendation is required (eg in the case of a remand for report), it must be given by a practitioner approved by the Secretary of State under section 12 'as having special experience in the diagnosis or treatment of mental disorder'. When two medical recommendations are required (eg in respect of a hospital or guardianship order, an interim hospital order, a remand for treatment or the transfer of a prisoner to hospital), the Act provides that at least one of them must be given by a practitioner approved by the Secretary of State under section 12 (s54(1)). The general provision in relation to Part II admissions that two doctors furnishing reports cannot be based at the same hospital does *not* apply to Part III.

If a medical report is submitted in evidence by the prosecution, a copy must be given to the accused person's representative. In cases where the accused person is not represented, the substance of the report must be disclosed to him or to his parent or guardian (s54(3)).

RESTRICTION ORDERS

Statutory authority: s41

Maximum duration of detention: without limit of time, or for a period specified by the court

Criterion: it appears to the court, 'having regard to the nature of the offence, the antecedents of the offender and the risk of his committing further offences if set at large', that it is necessary to impose a restriction order 'for the protection of the public from serious harm'

Procedure: can be imposed by a Crown Court when a hospital order has been made, if the evidence of at least one of the two medical practitioners whose recommendations are taken into account has been given orally

CROWN COURT

A Crown Court which has made a hospital order can also impose a restriction order if it considers, 'having regard to the nature of the offence, the antecedents of the offender and the risk of his committing further offences', that it is necessary to do so to protect the public from 'serious harm'. A restriction order cannot be made, however, unless one of the two medical recommendations is given orally in court.

MAGISTRATES' COURT

A Magistrates' Court cannot make a restriction order itself, but it can commit an offender over the age of 14 to a Crown Court so that a restriction order can be made (s43). If a Magistrates' Court is satisfied, on written or oral evidence, that appropriate arrangements have been made, it may order an offender to be admitted to hospital until his case is decided by the Crown Court (s44).

DURATION

A restriction order can be imposed without limit of time, or for a specified period. In the latter case, once the fixed term expires or otherwise ceases to have effect, the patient will still be liable to be detained under a hospital order *without* restrictions.

In *R v Gardiner [1967] 1 A11 ER 895*, a practice direction was given that restriction orders of fixed duration should only be made in exceptional cases where doctors are able to assert confidently that recovery will take place within a certain period. The great majority of restriction orders are made without limit of time.

If the Home Secretary is satisfied that a restriction order is no longer necessary to protect the public from serious harm, he can direct that the patient should cease to be subject to restrictions (s42). In cases where such a direction has been issued, the patient is liable to be detained under a hospital order *without* restrictions.

EFFECT

Once a Crown Court has imposed restrictions upon the patient's discharge, none of the provisions in Part II of the Act relating to duration, renewal and expiration of the authority to detain apply. The patient cannot be granted leave of absence, transferred or discharged by the RMO or the managers without the consent of the Home Secretary; the nearest relative does not have the power to order his discharge (s41). However, in order to implement the judgement of the European Court of Human Rights in *X v The United Kingdom*, the 1983 Act does authorise a Mental Health Review Tribunal to discharge restricted patients (see chapter 6).

ABSOLUTE DISCHARGE

A restricted patient can be discharged by the Home Secretary or by a Mental Health Review Tribunal. The Home Secretary or a MHRT can grant an absolute discharge, or may specify that the discharge is subject to conditions. If a patient is given an absolute discharge, both the hospital order and the restriction order cease to have effect, and he cannot be recalled to hospital.

CONDITIONAL DISCHARGE AND RECALL

If a patient's discharge is *conditional,* he may, for example, be directed to live in a specific place or to attend for treatment. A conditionally discharged patient can be recalled to hospital at any time while the restriction order is still in force, but if this happens he *must* be given the reasons for his recall under a two stage procedure introduced as a result of the decision of the European Commission in *X v The United Kingdom* (see Home Office circular 117/1980).

Under the first stage of this procedure, the officer who initially detains the patient must inform him that he is being recalled to hospital by the Home Secretary under section 42(3) of the Mental Health Act 1983. The second stage involves the medical staff of the hospital to which the patient is returned giving him a further detailed explanation of the reasons for the recall. The detaining officer must notify the patient that this further explanation will be forthcoming when he arrives at the hospital.

X v The United Kingdom

The effect of an order or direction restricting a patient's discharge from hospital was fundamentally altered by the Amendment Act as a result of a decision taken by the European Court of Human Rights. Under Article 5(4) of the European Convention on Human Rights, a person detained by reason of *unsoundness of mind* must have the right to a periodic judicial review of the justification for his detention. In the case of *X v The United Kingdom* (judgement given 5 November 1981), the European Court found that the Home Secretary's *exclusive* power to discharge a restricted patient was inconsistent with the requirements of Article 5(4). Furthermore, it held that the writ of *habeas corpus* was too narrow in scope to provide an adequate safeguard against a patient's unjustified detention.

A restricted patient detained in hospital can now apply to a MHRT which has the power to discharge him: under the 1959 Act MHRTs could only act in an advisory capacity in respect of the discharge of restricted patients. Mental Health Review Tribunals are discussed in detail in chapter 6 and see also Gostin, *Human rights, judicial review and the mentally disordered offender* (Criminal Law Review 779, 1982).

ANNUAL MEDICAL REVIEW

In order to monitor the progress of restricted patients, the 1983 Act introduces a requirement that the RMO must examine all such patients and furnish a report to the Home Secretary at intervals of not more than one year (s41(6)).

TRANSFERS FROM PRISON TO HOSPITAL

Statutory authority: s47

Maximum duration of detention: if no restriction direction is given, the maximum duration of detention is as for a hospital order without restrictions, ie six months, renewable for a further six months and then for periods of one year at a time; if a restriction direction *is* given, it continues in force until the earliest date on which the person would have been released from prison with remission; thereafter the person is detained under a hospital order without restrictions

Criteria: the Home Secretary must be satisfied that the prisoner is
(a) suffering from mental illness, psychopathic disorder, severe mental impairment or mental impairment; and
(b) the mental disorder is of a nature or degree which makes it appropriate for him to be detained in a hospital for medical treatment; and
(c) in the case of psychopathic disorder or mental impairment, treatment is 'likely to alleviate or prevent a deterioration of his condition'

Procedure: direction by the Home Secretary and reports from two registered medical practitioners

A person who is serving a sentence of imprisonment can be transferred to a hospital (but *not* a mental nursing home). The Home Secretary must be satisfied, on the basis of reports from two doctors, that the relevant criteria are fulfilled, and must also consider, 'having regard to the public interest and all the circumstances', that it is 'expedient' to transfer the prisoner.

A transfer direction has the same effect as a hospital order. If he thinks it necessary, the Home Secretary can make a transfer direction and also impose restrictions on the patient's discharge. The current practice is almost invariably to impose restrictions on a transferred prisoner, although exceptions are usually made in the case of prisoners transferred a month or less before their expected date of release from prison.

When a restriction direction is given in respect of a person transferred from prison to hospital, it continues in force until the earliest date on which the person would have been discharged from prison with remission. Thereafter the patient continues to be liable to detention under a hospital order without restrictions (s50). This provision was incorporated in the Amendment Act in response to a proposal made by MIND in **A Human Condition** (volume 2). Under the 1959 Act the restriction order did not lapse until a person's *total* sentence had expired. However, a prisoner can normally expect to be released from prison after serving two-thirds of his sentence, one-third having been removed as remission for good behaviour. Section 50 now specifies that a restriction direction ceases to have effect on the date on which the patient 'could have been discharged if he had not forfeited remission of any part of the sentence'.

It may become apparent during the course of the restriction direction that the offender no longer requires treatment in hospital for mental disorder, or that no effective treatment can be given. If the Home Secretary is notified that this is the case by the RMO or another doctor, or by a MHRT, he has two options: he can either discharge an offender who would have been eligible for release or parole, or he can direct that the person be returned to prison to serve the remainder of the sentence.

TRANSFER TO HOSPITAL OF PRISONERS WHO ARE NOT SERVING SENTENCES OF IMPRISONMENT

Statutory authority: s48

Maximum duration of detention: variable, depending upon the category of prisoner

Criterion: a person is suffering from mental illness or severe mental impairment 'of a nature or degree which makes it appropriate for him to be detained for medical treatment' and 'he is in urgent need of such treatment'

Procedure: direction by the Home Secretary and reports from two medical practitioners

A person who is detained in a prison or remand centre, but who is not serving a sentence of imprisonment, can be transferred to hospital on the direction of the Home Secretary. Civil prisoners and people detained under the Immigration Act 1971 can also be transferred to hospital. Before he makes a transfer direction, the Home Secretary must be satisfied, on the basis of reports from two doctors, that the relevant criterion is fulfilled.

A transfer direction has the same effect as a hospital order. The Home Secretary *must* (but in the case of a civil prisoner or a person detained under the Immigration Act *may*) also make a restriction direction (ss51,53).

SUMMARY

The provisions for the disposal of mentally disordered people concerned in criminal proceedings appear to be complex. However, they become easier to understand once it is appreciated that they all represent initiatives, at various stages of the criminal process, which seek to send a mentally disordered person to hospital rather than prison. Under English law, the provisions which may be used to divert a mentally disordered person from the criminal justice system to the mental health system are these –

(i)   **mental disorder at the time of the offence:** this includes lack of criminal responsibility *(the insanity defence)* or *diminished responsibility*. The former results in an automatic hospital order with restrictions, while the latter gives the judge discretion to pass whatever sentence he considers appropriate;

(ii) **mental disorder at the time of the trial:** this may result in a finding of *disability in relation to trial,* leading to an automatic hospital order with restrictions. At this stage the court can also opt to *remand a person to hospital for a report or for treatment;*

(iii) **mental disorder at the time of sentencing:** in this case, the court can make an *interim or full hospital order;*

(iv) **mental disorder after sentencing:** on the recommendation of two medical practitioners, the Home Secretary can *transfer* a person serving a sentence of imprisonment to hospital.

(See the table *Admission to hospital: Part III* on pp 85-90 for further explanation of these provisions.)

Before an offender who is found to be mentally disordered can be admitted to hospital, a consultant must usually be prepared to make a bed available. It is this practical difficulty, rather than a failing in the enabling provisions of English law, which often hinders the admission to hospital of mentally disordered offenders.

CHAPTER 6

MENTAL HEALTH REVIEW TRIBUNALS

Mental Health Review Tribunals (MHRTs) are independent bodies which were originally established under the 1959 Act. They hear applications and references by, or in respect of, patients detained or subject to guardianship under Parts II and III of the 1983 Act. Mental Health Review Tribunals are not to be confused with the Mental Health Act Commission. They are empowered to consider the need for continuing detention under the 1983 Act: they are not a forum for patients' complaints. There is a MHRT for every region covered by a Regional Health Authority in England, and one for Wales (s65). Four tribunal offices provide MHRTs throughout England and Wales with administrative support, and these are listed in Appendix III.

STRUCTURE

Tribunal members are drawn from panels of lawyers, medical practitioners, and lay people with experience in administration and knowledge of social services or other relevant qualifications or skills. All members are appointed by the Lord Chancellor (s65(2), schedule 2), and a practitioner from the legal panel is appointed chairman in each region.

Under the Act, a tribunal can comprise at least one member from the legal, medical and lay panels, with the legal member appointed president. In practice a tribunal usually has just three members: a lawyer (as president), a doctor, and a lay person with experience in administration or social services.

SPECIAL COMPOSITION OF TRIBUNALS HEARING RESTRICTED CASES

Throughout the Parliamentary debates on the Act, the Government expressed concern that the courts might not have confidence in MHRTs as a means of protecting the public interest. It was felt that this lack of confidence might result in some courts demonstrating reluctance to make a hospital order in the case of a mentally disordered offender convicted of a particularly serious offence. Accordingly, the Act provides that rules can be made to limit the tribunal members who are qualified to hear the cases of patients subject to restriction orders or directions. The MHRT president in these cases will be a lawyer with substantial experience in the criminal courts: this would normally be a circuit judge, but could also be a recorder.

However, circuit judges and recorders may, as ordinary members of the legal panel, also hear non-restricted cases, and indeed it was envisaged in the Parliamentary debates that they would do so on occasion.

PROCEDURE

MHRT proceedings are governed by the Mental Health Review Tribunal Rules 1983, SI 1983 no 942, promulgated by the Lord Chancellor (s78). For a detailed discussion of the Rules see L.O. Gostin, E. Rassaby & A. Buchan, **Mental Health Review Tribunals** (Oyez Longman, in press).

REPRESENTATION

Public finance from the legal aid fund became available to meet the cost of representation before MHRTs on 1 December 1982. Solicitors – but not lay representatives – are therefore eligible to apply for *Assistance by Way of Representation,* and the legal aid fund can also finance independent psychiatric or social enquiry reports on patients appearing before MHRTs. The addresses of area legal aid committees are included in Appendix III.

Both MIND and the Law Society operate a panel of representatives for patients applying to MHRTs.

APPLICATIONS & REFERENCES

A case can come before a Mental Health Review Tribunal in one of three ways: the patient or his nearest relative can make an application during specified periods; the Secretary of State for Social Services (or the Home Secretary for restricted patients) can refer a case to a tribunal at any time; if a case is not reviewed by a tribunal within specified periods, it is referred automatically.

APPLICATIONS

There are many circumstances in which a patient or his nearest relative can apply to a MHRT, and the tables on pp 45-46 give a comprehensive account of when and how applications can be made in respect of patients detained under Parts II and III of the Act. The most important periods of eligibility are these—

Admission for assessment (s2) – the *patient* can apply within the first 14 days of admission

Admission for treatment (s3) – the *patient* can apply within the first six months of admission and during each period of renewal, ie within the next six months and then annually. The *nearest relative* can *only* apply after his power to discharge the patient has been overruled by the RMO: he can apply within the period of 28 days after he has been informed that the RMO has issued a report barring the discharge

Reception into guardianship (s7) – the patient can apply within the first six months of reception, during the next six months and during each subsequent period of one year. The nearest relative does not have the right to apply to a tribunal because he can order the patient's discharge at any time and his discharge order cannot be barred by the RMO

Hospital order without restrictions (s37) – the patient *or* his nearest relative can apply in the period between six and twelve months after the making of the order, and in any subsquent period of one year

Restriction order or restriction direction – with certain exceptions, the *patient* can apply in the period between six and twelve months after the order is made, and in any subsequent period of one year

Guardianship order (s37) – the *patient* can apply within the first six months of the order, within the following six months, and during each subsequent period of one year. The nearest relative can apply within the first year of the order, and during each subsequent period of one year

In each case only one application can be made during the period specified. Applications may be withdrawn without prejudice to the applicant's rights within the eligibility period.

REFERENCES

The Secretary of State for Social Services may, 'if he thinks fit, at any time', refer to a MHRT the case of any patient who is liable to be detained or subject to guardianship under Part II of the Act (s67). The Home Secretary has the same right in respect of restricted patients (s71). However, these powers are rarely exercised. References are only likely to be made if, for example, important new evidence in relation to a patient's case has come to light since the previous tribunal hearing.

Automatic references

The 1983 Act imposes on the hospital managers the duty to refer to a MHRT the case of any patient who has been admitted for treatment and who has not had a tribunal hearing within the first six months of admission. Thereafter the managers must refer to a MHRT the case of any patient admitted for treatment or on a hospital order who has not had a tribunal hearing during the previous three years (one year if a child under the age of 16 is concerned) (s68). The Home Secretary is also required to refer the case of a restricted patient if it has not been reviewed by a MHRT within the previous three years (s71(2)).

The Secretary of State for Social Services and the Home Secretary have the power to make an order varying the periods of time specified in these sections (ss68(4), 71(3)).

POWERS OF TRIBUNALS

UNRESTRICTED PATIENTS

Discharge

A MHRT *may* discharge a patient who is liable to be detained under the Mental Health Act, and has a general right to exercise this discretion in the case of unrestricted patients. A tribunal has a *duty* to discharge unrestricted patients if certain statutory criteria are met. These criteria vary according to whether the patient was admitted for assessment (s72(1)(a)), or whether he was admitted for treatment or is under a hospital order without restrictions (s72(1)(b)). A tribunal also has the power to discharge a patient from guardianship (s72(4)).

It is worth observing that a tribunal is not *obliged* to discharge a patient who was admitted for treatment or who is under a hospital order even if the *treatability requirement* is not met; the tribunal must only 'have regard' to the treatability of the patient.

Delayed discharge

A tribunal can direct that a patient be discharged on a future date so that there is adequate time for appropriate after-care arrangements to be made. This provision was introduced by the Amendment Act because under the 1959 Act patients had to be discharged *immediately* the MHRT had reached a decision – often before suitable after-care had been arranged.

Recommendation for transfer or leave of absence

If a tribunal feels that a patient is not yet ready to be discharged it can – 'with a view to facilitating his discharge on a future date' – recommend that he be granted a leave of absence, or transferred to another hospital or into guardianship. The MHRT can further consider the patient's case if the hospital does not comply with its recommendations (s72(3)).

A tribunal can also direct that a patient's condition be reclassified to another form of mental disorder (s72(5)).

POWER TO DISCHARGE RESTRICTED PATIENTS

A MHRT must order that a restricted patient be given either an *absolute* or a *conditional* discharge if the statutory criteria are fulfilled: in the latter case the tribunal can *defer* the direction for conditional discharge until the necessary arrangements have been made (s73).

In the case of a patient who has been transferred from prison to hospital with a restriction direction, the tribunal has to decide whether he would be entitled to an absolute or a conditional discharge. If he would be entitled to a conditional discharge, the tribunal must recommend whether he should stay in hospital or be returned to prison. These provisions are designed to help the Home Secretary decide whether the patient should be discharged, kept in hospital or transferred back to prison.

As the Act now stands, a tribunal technically has no power to recommend a transfer or leave of absence. This was an unintended omission, and the DHSS recognises that tribunals may wish to make such recommendations. The possibility of a transfer is particularly important for restricted patients in special hospitals who often need to spend some time in the less restrictive surroundings of a local hospital as part of their gradual preparation for returning to life in the community.

PART II PATIENTS

Category of admission etc	Application		Automatic reference by the hospital managers (s68)
	Patient	Nearest relative	
Admission for assessment (s2)	Within the first 14 days of admission	—	—
Admission for treatment (s3)	Within the first six months of admission, during the next six months, and during each subsequent period of one year	Within 28 days after being informed that RMO has issued a report barring nearest relative from discharging patient	If MHRT has not reviewed case within the first six months of admission; thereafter, if MHRT has not considered case within period of three years (one year for child under the age of 16)
Reception into guardianship (s7)	Within the first six months of reception, during the next six months, and during each subsequent period of one year	—	—
Reclassification of patient as suffering from a different form of mental disorder (s16)	Within 28 days after being informed of the reclassification	Within 28 days after the reclassification (application can be made by patient or nearest relative	—
Patient transferred from guardianship to hospital (s19)	Within six months of the day on which the patient is transferred	—	If MHRT has not reviewed case within first six months of transfer; thereafter, if MHRT has not considered case within period of three years
Nearest relative displaced by County Court (s29)	—	Within one year after County Court orders displacement of nearest relative and subsequently in each period of one year for which order is in force	—

PART III PATIENTS

Category of admission	Application		Automatic reference by the hospital managers (s68) or the Home Secretary (s71(2))
	Patient	Nearest relative	
Hospital order without restrictions (s37)	Between six and twelve months after the making of the order, and during each subsequent period of one year	Between six and twelve months after the making of the order, and during each subsequent period of one year	Reference by managers if a period of three years has elapsed since case was last considered by MHRT (one year for child under the age of 16)
Guardianship order (s37)	Within the first six months of the guardianship order, during the next six months, and during each subsequent period of one year	Within one year of the guardianship order, and during each subsequent period of one year	—
Certain cases where hospital order is made but court does not make a specific determination that admission to hospital is necessary, eg if restriction order ceases to have effect, or if hospital order with restrictions is made following a finding under Criminal Procedure (Insanity) Act 1964	Within six months of the date of the hospital order or direction, during the next six months, and during each subsequent period of one year	Between six and twelve months after the making of the order, and during each subsequent period of one year	Reference by managers if case has not been reviewed by MHRT within first six months; thereafter if case has not been considered by MHRT within three years (one year for child under the age of 16)
Patient with restriction order or restriction direction (defined s79) who is in hospital	Between six and twelve months after the making of the order or direction, and during each subsequent period of one year	—	Reference by Home Secretary in respect of any case not considered by MHRT within the last three years
Restricted patient who has been conditionally discharged and is recalled to hospital (s42, and see s75)	As if restriction order were made afresh on date of recall	As if restriction order were made afresh on date of recall	Reference by Home Secretary within one month after recall
Restricted patient who has been conditionally discharged and not recalled (s42, and see s75)	Between one and two years after conditional discharge, and during each subsequent period of two years	—	—

46

CHAPTER 7
CONSENT TO TREATMENT

Under the 1959 Act, the legal position of a detained patient who wished to refuse treatment was unclear. The legislation authorised compulsory admission if treatment was 'warranted'; however, it failed to specify whether that which was warranted could actually be imposed. It had been widely assumed that if a person was compulsorily admitted to hospital for treatment he was incompetent to decide whether or not he should be given treatment. This assumption is no longer valid, and Part IV of the 1983 Act introduces a number of statutory provisions which must be enforced when a detained patient refuses treatment. These provisions are complicated, and must be read in conjunction with the regulations issued by the Secretary of State for Social Services (Mental Health (Hospital, Guardianship and Consent to Treatment) Regulations 1983, no 893, reg 16) and the code of practice. The Mental Health Act Commission will submit proposals for the code of practice to the Secretary of State who will be responsible for consulting on them.

PATIENTS TO WHOM PART IV APPLIES

Part IV of the Act applies to all patients who are 'liable to be detained' except those detained for short periods (eg under emergency admission, doctor's or nurse's holding power, police power or removal by warrant), and those remanded to hospital for report. In addition, the provisions do not apply to restricted patients who are conditionally discharged from hospital or patients subject to guardianship. Patients who are outside the scope of Part IV have the same right to refuse treatment as an informal patient in a mental illness or mental handicap hospital or a patient admitted to a general hospital with a physical disorder.

Part IV applies only to medical treatment for mental disorder given under the direction of the RMO, and *not* to treatment administered solely in order to alleviate a physical disorder (eg an appendectomy), or for social purposes (eg a nontherapeutic sterilisation).

In sum, Part IV of the Act does not apply to informal patients or to those who are detained for 72 hours or less, remanded for report, under guardianship or conditionally discharged. *These patients have the same right to refuse treatment as any other patient under common law.* Since the great majority of patients in hospital are admitted informally, it is useful to examine in detail their common law right to refuse treatment.

RIGHTS OF PATIENTS UNDER COMMON LAW

Historically, the common law has protected the personal and bodily interests of the individual through a tort known in law as *trespass of the person.* The administration of treatment to a person without his consent constitutes *battery* and is actionable; apprehension of physical treatment without consent (ie if a person *believes* that he is about to have imposed upon him a physical treatment he does not want) is an *assault.* The law of trespass upholds the common law principle that each person should be able to make his own decisions about his well-being; even if the proposed treatment is likely to benefit the patient, it will still be a case of battery unless the patient gives his consent or the treatment is urgently necessary.

Consent may be either given expressly, or implied by conduct. Express consent may be given orally or in writing, but a signed consent form does not in itself constitute consent; it is merely evidence of consent which can be negatived, for example by proof of duress or incompetency. A patient's consent can be inferred from his behaviour if he presents himself to a doctor and does not verbally or physically resist treatment which is ordinarily and reasonably expected within the boundaries of the doctor/patient relationship – for example, putting an arm out for an injection.

Consent, be it express or implied, can be withdrawn at any time before or during the medical treatment or examination.

A valid consent is usually an amalgamation of a number of elements—

- *Information* – the patient must be told about the nature and purpose of the treatment, and about any serious side-effects, although he need not be informed of every minor risk or possible adverse effect. If the patient wants more information, he is entitled to ask for it, and the doctor must answer truthfully

- *Competency* – the patient must be able to understand the nature and purpose of the treatment. Mental disorder does not automatically render a person incompetent; indeed, a patient's competency is likely to vary over time and according to the nature of the decision to be taken. A young person between the ages of 16 and 18 can give and withhold consent as if he were an adult, but there is no clear legal opinion about the validity of a consent given by a child under the age of 16. The preferred view is that the consent is valid as long as the child is competent to understand the nature and purpose of the treatment

- *Voluntariness* – the patient must give his consent without being subject to coercion or unreasonable influence. Consent is invalidated if it is extracted under duress or as the result of fraud or deceit.

THE NON-VOLITIONAL PATIENT

If one of these elements is missing, there is no valid consent and the treatment may constitute a technical battery; unhappily, this leaves a great vacuum in English law. There are many informal patients who are incompetent to give consent to medical or psychiatric treatment, for example patients who are severely mentally ill, severely mentally handicapped or elderly and confused. Situations arise where highly vulnerable, isolated and withdrawn patients require beneficial medical treatment (such as the removal of a cataract) to which they cannot give consent. Strictly speaking, it would not be lawful to treat such a patient except in a case of urgent necessity; a court order might be required to establish the legal position for certain.

Staff faced with this situation are given no official guidance in law or in departmental circulars. The most sensible advice for them would be to proceed only if there is complete agreement on the need for treatment. They should obtain the consent of the nearest relative, although this has no validity in law. The patient, of course, should be kept informed and consulted to the greatest possible extent.

URGENT NECESSITY

Under the common law, treatment can be given without the consent of the patient in cases of *necessity*. The doctrine of necessity is not clearly defined in law, but it would obviously encompass the use of a life-saving treatment performed when the patient could not provide consent (eg by reason of unconsciousness), but was not known to object to the treatment. Indeed, the doctrine of necessity might be construed more liberally to embrace treatment or restraint administered in the course of an emergency – for example, a tranquilliser injected to calm a patient during a violent episode. An emergency is taken to mean a circumstance in which immediate action is necessary to preserve life, or to prevent a serious and immediate danger to the patient or other people. In such a case the treatment or physical restraint used would have to be reasonable and sufficient only to the purpose of bringing the emergency to an end. It would be unwise for a nurse or any other medically unqualified person to administer medical treatment except under the specific direction of a registered medical practitioner.

TREATMENT GIVEN UNDER PART IV OF THE ACT

The Act establishes several categories of treatment, each with specific legal safeguards. A patient to whom Part IV applies is not required to give consent to any treatment for mental disorder given by the RMO which falls outside these categories (s63). (It is, however, sound professional practice to consult the patient and his nearest relative in every case, and to seek their agreement to any treatment programme.)

TREATMENT REQUIRING CONSENT AND A SECOND OPINION

Statutory authority: s57

Treatments: (a) psychosurgery; and
(b) treatments specified in regulations issued by the Secretary of State for Social Services (ie surgical implantation of hormones); and
(c) treatments identified in a code of practice as giving rise to special concern (s118(2)) (no treatments yet specified)

Requirements: treatment cannot be given unless the patient consents and a second opinion agrees—
  (i) the consent must be confirmed by a doctor (not the RMO) and two other people (*not* doctors) appointed by the MHAC. They must certify in writing that the patient understands the nature, purpose and likely effects of the treatment, and has consented to it;
 (ii) the doctor appointed by the MHAC must certify in writing that, 'having regard to the likelihood of the treatment alleviating or preventing a deterioration of the patient's condition', the treatment should be given;
(iii) before issuing a certificate the doctor must consult two other people who have been concerned with the patient's treatment, one a nurse and the other neither a nurse nor a doctor

Special application: the provisions of section 57 apply to informal patients as well as detained patients covered by Part IV of the Act

The regulations referred to in Part IV of the Act are drafted by the Secretary of State for Social Services in consultation with relevant bodies. The code of practice mentioned in section 118 is to be prepared by the Secretary of State in consultation with the MHAC; in practice, the Commission is expected to prepare it. This code differs from the regulations in that it will not have quite the same binding statutory effect. Nevertheless, professionals will be expected to abide by the provisions of the code, and the MHAC will monitor the extent to which it is put into practice.

THE TREATMENTS (PSYCHOSURGERY AND SEX HORMONE IMPLANTS)

The provisions of section 57 so far refer to psychosurgery and sex hormone implant treatments. Psychosurgery is administered in approximately 100-200 cases per year in England and Wales, and is used primarily in the treatment of severe depression and other affective disorders. It is considered a controversial treatment on a number of counts: it is irreversible; the cerebral sites destroyed vary widely; and it is occasionally used in circumstances where there is little evidence for its efficacy, for example to control aggressive behaviour. See Gostin, *Psychosurgery: a hazardous and unestablished treatment? A case for the importation of American legal safeguards to Great Britain* (Journal of Social Welfare Law 83, March 1982).

Sex hormone implant treatments are rarely administered in psychiatric hospitals today, but one example of their use is given in **A Human Condition** (volume 2), pp89-90. The usual object of this treatment is to modify the sexual urges of patients with a history of sexual assault.

The regulations do not appear to control the use of hormones administered orally rather than by surgical implantation.

THE PROCEDURES

Psychosurgery or sex hormone implant treatment cannot be administered to any patient without—
(i) a multidisciplinary certificate from three professionals (only one of whom is a doctor) appointed by the MHAC confirming the patient's consent; *and*
(ii) a second opinion by a doctor appointed by the MHAC confirming the appropriateness of the treatment.

Before giving the second opinion, the independent doctor must consult two other people who have been concerned with the patient's treatment (eg two members of the therapeutic team), one a nurse and the other neither a nurse nor a doctor.

A section 57 treatment thus requires both the patient's consent *and* a second opinion: it is virtually the only provision in English law which stipulates that, even if the patient consents, treatment cannot be administered unless there is *independent* verification that the patient is competent to give his consent and that the treatment is effective. The state therefore has the right to intervene in cases where the doctor and patient agree on the need for a medically recognised treatment.

The justification for interfering with the voluntary therapeutic relationship between doctor and patient is that these particular treatments give rise to special concern since they may be irreversible, unusually hazardous, or insufficiently established. For these reasons, Parliament decided that section 57 should apply to informal as well as detained patients.

TREATMENT REQUIRING CONSENT OR A SECOND OPINION

Statutory authority: s58

Treatments: (a) treatments specified in regulations (ie ECT); and
(b) medication, but only three months after it is first administered

Requirements: treatment cannot be given unless the patient consents *or* a second opinion agrees—
 (i) the RMO or a doctor appointed by the MHAC must certify in writing that the patient is capable of understanding the 'nature, purpose and likely effects' of the treatment and has consented to it; or
 (ii) a doctor appointed by the MHAC (not the RMO) must certify in writing that 'the patient is not capable of understanding the nature, purpose and likely effects of that treatment or has not consented to it but that, having regard to the likelihood of its alleviating or preventing a deterioration of his condition, the treatment should be given';
(iii) before giving the certificate the independent doctor must consult two other people who have been professionally concerned with the patient's medical treatment, one a nurse and the other neither a nurse nor a doctor

THE THREE MONTHS RULE

Treatments so far covered by section 58 are electroconvulsive therapy (ECT), and medication *after* it has been administered for a period of three months. The *three months rule* means that medication can be administered for three months without the consent of the patient or a second opinion. The period of three months commences when medication is first administered 'during a period for which he (the patient) is liable to be detained as a patient to whom this Part of this Act applies'. For example, if medication is administered to an informal patient or one who is detained for a period of up to 72 hours, the three month period does not come into operation. It only commences once the patient concerned has been detained under a section which falls within the scope of Part IV, for example admission for assessment or treatment.

The Secretary of State for Social Services has the power to vary the period of time specified in section 58.

It is important to know whether the particular form of medication to be administered has been specified in the regulations or the code of practice. There are three possibilities—

(a) it may be specified in the *regulations or code of practice as a treatment for which consent *and* a second opinion are required;
(b) it may be specified in the *regulations as a treatment requiring consent *or* a second opinion: in this case the three months rule would not apply, and the

---

* No form of medication is specified in the current regulations.

51

provisions of section 58 should be observed *before* the medication is first given;

(c) if, as will usually be the case, a particular medication is not specified in the regulations or the code of practice, the requirements of section 58 only apply after three months have elapsed since the medication was first given 'during a period for which (the patient) is liable to be detained' as a patient to whom Part IV of the Act applies.

THE PROCEDURES

Treatment can be administered under section 58 in one of two ways—

(1) the patient must consent and a certificate must be given by the RMO or a doctor appointed by the MHAC confirming the validity of his consent;
or

(2) if the patient refuses to give his consent or is incapable of doing so, a doctor appointed by the MHAC must give a second opinion on the appropriateness of the treatment. Before giving this second opinion, the independent doctor must consult two other people who have been professionally concerned with the patient's treatment, one a nurse and the other neither a nurse nor a doctor.

Section 58 represents a fundamental departure from traditional common law assumptions in that it specifies circumstances in which treatment can be imposed upon a patient who is competent to understand the nature and purpose of the treatment, but refuses to give his consent. Good professional practice dictates that the patient's consent should always be sought, and alternative treatments explored and discussed with the patient and his nearest relative. Members of the therapeutic team who may be consulted by the independent doctor should ensure that the fullest possible discussions have taken place. If the patient is competent and expressly refuses the treatment, it should only be imposed when there is substantial justification relating to the person's health. For further discussion of this issue see Gostin, *Compulsory treatment in psychiatry: some reflections on self-determination, patient competency and professional expertise* (Poly Law Review 86, 1982) and Gostin, *Observations on consent to treatment and review of clinical judgement in psychiatry: a discussion paper* (Journal of the Royal Society of Medicine 742, 1981).

THE DUTY TO CONSULT

It is interesting that under Part IV the doctor giving a second opinion is required *by law* to consult with members of the multidisciplinary team. The professionals who are consulted have no formal powers to influence the independent doctor's second opinion, although they should report irregularities to the MHAC.

This provision was introduced to promote good professional practice by requiring doctors to have discussions with other members of the multidisciplinary team.

PLANS OF TREATMENT

Any consent or certificate given under Part IV can apply to a single form of treatment, or to a plan of treatment (s59). There is scope for a great deal of flexibility and variation in the way a plan of treatment is framed: it can include several forms of treatment (although only forms of treatment which fall into the same category); it can specify the circumstances in which a particular treatment can be given (eg the dosage of medication); and it can (and, arguably, *should)* set a time limit on the duration of the treatment programme. A further second opinion must be given in accordance with the particular section if treatment is administered outside of the terms of the plan of treatment.

WITHDRAWAL OF CONSENT

Under common law, a patient can withdraw his consent at any time before or during the administration of treatment. The patient's right to withdraw his consent is affirmed by section 60, although exception is made for cases of urgency (see below). Consent can be withdrawn to a particular treatment in a plan, or to the plan in its entirety.

If the RMO proposes that the treatment be reintroduced after the patient has withdrawn his consent, the procedures required under the relevant section must be started afresh. Should the patient then decide to give consent, he still has the right to withdraw it again if he chooses. However, the RMO has the power to continue with treatment when consent has been withdrawn if he considers that 'discontinuance . . . would cause serious suffering to the patient' (s62(2)).

REVIEW OF TREATMENT

During the House of Commons Standing Committee on the Mental Health (Amendment) Bill, the Minister for Health expressed the concern that 'it would be theoretically possible as a matter of law for someone to obtain an open-ended second opinion' – ie a second opinion which did not specify any limit of time. Thus a treatment could in theory be continued indefinitely without the patient having the right to obtain a further second opinion. As a result of this concern, the Mental Health Act makes provision for a continuing review of all treatments given in accordance with sections 57 and 58.

The RMO must furnish the Secretary of State for Social Services with a report on the treatment and the patient's condition at the time the patient's detention is renewed, and at any other time the Secretary of State requires (s61). Moreover, the Secretary of State can at any time give the RMO notice that, subject to the provisions in relation to urgent treatment, a certificate is void, and a further certificate is required if treatment is to be continued (s61(3)).

The MHAC will undertake the responsibilities of the Secretary of State in all of these respects (s121).

URGENT TREATMENT

Any treatment to which Part IV of the Act applies can be administered without the need for consent or a second opinion if it is urgent (s62). Urgent treatment is defined as treatment which is—
(a) immediately necessary to save the patient's life; or
(b) (not being irreversible), immediately necessary to prevent a serious deterioration of his condition; or
(c) (not being irreversible or hazardous), immediately necessary to alleviate serious suffering by the patient; or
(d) (not being irreversible or hazardous), immediately necessary and represents

the minimum interference necessary to prevent the patient from behaving violently or being a danger to himself or to others.

Section 62 only comes into force in urgent situations where treatment is *immediately necessary;* treatment without consent or a second opinion cannot be justified simply because it is necessary or would be beneficial. Urgent treatment cannot be continued beyond the point at which the crisis has been brought to an end, and the usual safeguards provided in Part IV should then be observed.

The definition of urgent treatment means that, in certain circumstances, treatments which are irreversible or hazardous cannot be administered without the appropriate consent and/or second opinion, *even* if they are urgently necessary. The Act defines the terms *irreversible* and *hazardous* in a somewhat circular fashion: 'treatment is irreversible if it has unfavourable irreversible physical or psychological consequences and hazardous if it entails significant physical hazard' (s62(3)). The Department of Health and Social Security considers that the decision as to whether a particular treatment is irreversible or hazardous is, in the first instance, a matter for the RMO. However, the RMO must make decisions which are reasonable and within the mainstream of contemporary medical thought.

The scope of the urgency provisions in Part IV of the Act is wider than that of the doctrine of *necessity* in common law. It is therefore important to recognise that they apply only to patients who come within the remit of Part IV and not, for example, to informal patients or patients on short-term compulsory admission sections. The legal position of patients in these latter categories is described in detail on pp 48-49.

OVERVIEW

The consent to treatment provisions in Part IV of the Act are complex, and it may therefore be useful to summarise the main principles and safeguards in a highly simplified step by step guide—

STEP 1: IDENTIFY THE LEGAL STATUS OF PATIENT

As a general rule, patients compulsorily admitted to hospital for up to 28 days or longer come within the scope of Part IV of the Act; informal patients, patients detained for up to 72 hours and guardianship patients do not. If the provisions of Part IV do not apply, the patient has the same legal rights as a patient receiving treatment for a physical disorder and, generally speaking, he can refuse treatment. (Remember that *all* patients for whom psychosurgery or sex hormone implant treatment is proposed come within the scope of Part IV.)

STEP 2: IDENTIFY THE TREATMENT

Category 1: psychosurgery and sex hormone implant treatment

Category 2: medication *after* it has been administered for three months, and ECT

Category 3: any other treatment for mental disorder administered under the direction of the RMO. (For non-psychiatric treatments, the common law rules apply; treatment for mental disorder includes nursing)

STEP 3: APPLY THE SAFEGUARD ACCORDING TO THE CATEGORY OF TREATMENT

Category 1: (i) *consent,* the validity of which must be confirmed by a certificate signed by three people appointed by the MHAC (only one a doctor); *and*

    (ii) *a second opinion* as to the appropriateness of the treatment from a doctor appointed by the MHAC;

    (iii) before giving the second opinion the doctor must *consult* with two other people on the therapeutic team, one a nurse and the other neither a nurse nor a doctor

Category 2: (i) *consent,* the validity of which must be confirmed by a certificate signed by the RMO or a doctor appointed by the MHAC; *or*

    (ii) *a second opinion* as to the appropriateness of the treatment from a doctor appointed by the MHAC;

    (iii) before giving the second opinion the doctor must *consult* with two other people on the therapeutic team, one a nurse and the other neither a nurse nor a doctor

Category 3: The patient can be treated without consent or a second opinion

Appendix II includes a flow chart which summarises the provisions relating to consent to treatment (see p 91).

CHAPTER 8

THE MENTAL HEALTH ACT COMMISSION

BACKGROUND

Throughout the history of mental health legislation there has been a number of bodies with the authority to review the exercise of compulsory powers as well as the treatment and care of mentally disordered people. The Lunatics Act 1845 established the Lunacy Commission which had a full-time inspectorate and a central secretariat. Commissioners were appointed by the Lord Chancellor and had the power to investigate and supervise standards in institutions, and to visit patients. The Lunacy Commission was reconstituted in 1913 as the Board of Control and given the additional responsibility of scrutinising documents relating to compulsory admission. The Board also had the power to order the discharge of detained patients.

The Mental Health Act 1959 abolished the Board of Control and its responsibilities have been redistributed. The duty to supervise conditions in hospitals is vested in the Health Advisory Service (in respect of mental illness hospitals) and the National Development Teams for the Mentally Handicapped; the power of discharge is vested in Mental Health Review Tribunals; the function of scrutinising documents relating to compulsory admission is vested in the hospital managers (the District Health Authorities in respect of local NHS hospitals and the Secretary of State for Social Services for the special hospitals); and the responsibility for investigating complaints is vested in the Health Service Commissioner (the Ombudsman).

Scotland also abolished the General Board of Control in the Mental Health (Scotland) Act 1960, but established in its place the Mental Welfare Commission. This body has a general duty to protect the rights of people who are mentally disordered, and its responsibilities are reviewed in detail in **The Mental Health Year Book 1981/82**. It is interesting to observe that a body equivalent to the Mental Welfare Commission has been proposed for Northern Ireland.

THE ESTABLISHMENT OF THE MENTAL HEALTH ACT COMMISSION

Section 121 of the Mental Health Act 1983 imposes upon the Secretary of State for Social Services the duty to establish (under section 11 of the National Health Service Act 1977) a special health authority known as the Mental Health Act Commission (MHAC). The MHAC has a general responsibility to protect the rights of detained patients: it is to keep under review the exercise of the compulsory powers and duties conferred by the Mental Health Act.

In addition, the Secretary of State has the power to direct the MHAC to keep under review the care and treatment of informal patients (s121(4)). However, he has yet to exercise this power, so the MHAC has no jurisdiction in respect of informal patients. The MHAC can ask the Secretary of State to extend its jurisdiction to informal patients, and before taking a decision on this matter he must consult relevant bodies.

The MHAC has responsibilities which may overlap with those of certain other bodies. However, the establishment of the MHAC is not intended to override or interfere with existing machinery for examining the care and treatment of patients. Thus, patients – be they informal or detained – can still refer complaints to the Health Service Commissioner or the hospital managers, and the Health Advisory Service and the National Development Teams will continue to investigate conditions in hospitals.

COMPOSITION AND FUNCTIONS

The MHAC will comprise 80-90 part-time members drawn from the medical, nursing, psychology, social work and legal professions, as well as lay people. Members will be appointed for varying periods of up to four years initially. The order establishing the MHAC and the relevant regulations do not prescribe a fixed number of members, so the figure of 80-90 can be adjusted if this proves to be necessary (see SI 1983 nos 892 and 894). The MHAC has a chairman and vice-chairman, and the Secretary of State has appointed a small central policy committee from amongst the membership. This committee will undertake a number of tasks, including drawing up proposals for the code of practice for submission to the Secretary of State on behalf of, and in consultation with, the Commission as a whole.

The MHAC has few actual powers – for example, it cannot discharge patients. Nonetheless, in most circumstances it reports *directly* to the Secretary of State who has the power under the Mental Health Act and the National Health Service Act 1977 to hold a health authority in default of its duties; ultimately the Secretary of State can dissolve a health authority and reconstitute it with different members. The success of the MHAC will depend to a large extent upon the abilities of its members and their willingness to uphold patients' rights and to adopt an innovative approach.

VISITING AND INTERVIEWING PATIENTS

The MHAC must make arrangements for its members to visit and interview patients in private (s120). It is envisaged that there will be one or two visits a year to each detained patient in the 300+ local hospitals and mental nursing homes throughout England and Wales, with approximately one visit a month to each of the four special hospitals.

INVESTIGATION OF COMPLAINTS

The MHAC must investigate two kinds of complaint (s120)—

(1) Complaints made by detained patients

The MHAC must make arrangements to investigate any complaint made by a patient about a matter which occurred while he was detained under the Act. This kind of complaint must be made *by the patient himself,* either during his detention or later. It need not be a complaint about the exercise of powers conferred by the Mental Health Act; incidents concerning alleged maltreatment, misappropriation of personal property etc can also be drawn to the attention of the MHAC.

Any complaint in this category must first be made to the hospital managers. The MHAC will investigate if they consider that the managers did not deal with the complaint satisfactorily.

(2) Complaints about the exercise of compulsory powers

The MHAC can make arrangements to investigate any complaint directly concerning the exercise of powers or duties conferred by the Act in respect of detained patients. This means that *any person* can complain to the MHAC on behalf of a detained patient about issues such as the alleged misuse of powers relating to compulsory detention under Part II or III, or consent to treatment under Part IV. This second category of complaint can be brought directly to the MHAC without first being referred to the managers. If a Member of Parliament asks for the investigation of a complaint which falls into this category, the results must be reported to him.

In summary then, the MHAC will investigate two kinds of complaint. A patient is entitled to draw the attention of the MHAC to any incident, however trivial, which occurs during his detention; the complaint need not relate directly to the provisions of the Mental Health Act. Such complaints must first be brought to the hospital managers. The other kind of complaint specifically concerns the exercise of compulsory powers in respect of patients detained under the Act. Complaints which fall into this category can be made by anyone, and need not first be referred to the managers. If such a complaint is brought by an MP, he must be given a report on the results of the investigation.

The MHAC can decide not to investigate, or to discontinue investigating, any complaint or part of a complaint. It may be, for example, that a complaint relates purely to clinical judgement or involves allegations of maladministration. There is nothing to stop the MHAC investigating such complaints as long as they fall within its jurisdiction, but the Commission may decide that it would be more appropriate for the matter to be dealt with by the Ombudsman or through the special procedures for reviewing complaints involving clinical judgement.

Any person investigating a complaint on behalf of the MHAC has the right to visit and interview a patient in private, and can demand to inspect records relating to the patient's detention or treatment.

It will be implicit in this description of its responsibilities that the MHAC does not replace existing authorities with a mandate to deal with complaints, for example the Health Service Commissioner and the Parliamentary Commissioner. For a review of existing complaints machinery see **Mental Health Services and the Law** (5th edition).

APPOINTING DOCTORS AND OTHER PERSONS

The MHAC is responsible for appointing medical practitioners and other persons to verify a patient's consent to treatment or to provide a second opinion under Part IV of the Act (see chapter 7). The MHAC can appoint its own members for this purpose, or it can choose from outside its ranks. Given that a large number of second opinions may well be needed, it is likely that the MHAC will be drawing from appropriate practitioners outside, as well as its own members.

REVIEW OF TREATMENT

The RMO has a duty to furnish the Secretary of State with regular reports regarding the continuation of treatment administered on the basis of a second opinion under Part IV of the Act (see chapter 7). The MHAC receives and examines these reports (s121), and it can render a second opinion void on behalf of the Secretary of State if it is not satisfied with the RMO's report.

CODE OF PRACTICE

Section 118 requires the Secretary of State for Social Services to prepare a code of practice including guidance in respect of compulsory admission and treatment. Amongst its other provisions, the code will supplement the regulations by listing treatments which should only be administered with the consent of the patient *and* a second opinion (see chapter 7).

The MHAC will be responsible for preparing the code, subject to the Secretary of State's approval: concerned bodies must be consulted during the drafting process. The code must be placed before Parliament, and either House can pass a resolution within 40 days requiring that it be withdrawn.

The code of practice does not have the same binding force as the regulations, but it is expected that practitioners will comply with its provisions.

CORRESPONDENCE

Under section 134 of the Act, post sent to, or by, a patient can be withheld in certain circumstances (see pp 60-61). If requested to do so, the MHAC can review any decision to withhold post, and it has the power to compel the managers to forward any correspondence or postal packet.

PUBLICATION OF REPORTS

The MHAC must publish a report on its activities in its second year of operation, and then bi-annually. A copy of the report must be laid before Parliament by the Secretary of State.

CHAPTER 9
IN-PATIENT RIGHTS

The principle underlying the Mental Health Act 1959 was that patients in mental illness and mental handicap hospitals should enjoy exactly the same rights as any other patient using a National Health Service facility. This principle is confirmed and extended in the 1983 Act. Informal patients retain almost all their rights of citizenship. In particular, informal patients' correspondence can no longer be withheld; they have the right to vote, subject to their capacity to make a statutory declaration; and, in general, they retain the right of unimpeded access to the courts. Their rights in other respects – for example, receiving visitors, making complaints and keeping clothing and personal possessions – should be no different from those of any patient having treatment for a physical illness in a general hospital.

As far as possible, compulsorily detained patients should also enjoy the same rights as any other patient: indeed, one of the assumptions behind the Percy Committee report and the Mental Health Act 1959 was that no distinction should be made between mental hospital patients on the basis of their legal status. In the main, this principle is upheld, but there are certain provisions in the Mental Health Act 1983 and in other legislation which affect only detained patients.

CORRESPONDENCE

The provisions in the Act vary according to whether the patient is informal or detained, or in a special hospital.

INFORMAL PATIENTS

Post sent to, or by, an informal patient cannot be read or withheld.

DETAINED PATIENTS IN LOCAL NHS HOSPITALS

Post sent *by* a detained patient in a local NHS hospital can be withheld only if the addressee has requested that communications addressed to him by the patient should be withheld (s134(1)(a)). Post sent *to* a detained patient may not be read or withheld.

SPECIAL HOSPITAL PATIENTS

There are particular provisions in respect of post sent to or from a patient detained in a special hospital.

Under section 134(1) post sent *by* a patient in a special hospital may be withheld from the Post Office if—

(a) the addressee has requested that communications addressed to him by the patient should be withheld; or
(b) the hospital managers consider that the communication is likely to cause *distress* to the addressee or to any other person (not being a person on the hospital staff); or
(c) the hospital managers consider that it is likely to cause *danger* to any person.

Post sent *to* a patient in a special hospital may be withheld if, in the opinion of the hospital managers, 'it is necessary to do so in the interests of the safety of the patient or for the protection of other persons' (s134(2)).

The special hospitals are managed by the Secretary of State for Social Services. (In the case of Rampton, most of the Secretary of State's responsibilities are delegated to the Rampton Hospital Board.) The Secretary of State can appoint a member of the special hospital staff to discharge his responsibilities in respect of patients' correspondence.

OPENING OF CORRESPONDENCE

The managers can open and inspect any correspondence in order to determine whether it should be withheld (s134(4)). When post has been opened, a record must be made and placed in the postal packet before it is resealed. The facts which must be noted in the record vary according to whether the packet or its contents were actually withheld or not. They always include the name of the person opening the packet and, if an item was not passed to the patient, the grounds on which it was withheld. See the Mental Health (Hospital, Guardianship and Consent to Treatment) Regulations 1983, no 893, regs 17-18.

REVIEW PROCESS

When post is withheld, the patient and/or the person who sent it must be notified within seven days. Those receiving such a notice can, within the next six months, ask the MHAC to review the decision to withhold the correspondence.

PRIVILEGED CORRESPONDENCE

Most of the provisions allowing post to be withheld do not apply if the correspondence is sent to, or by, any of the following—

(a) a Minister or MP
(b) the Court of Protection or the Lord Chancellor's Visitors
(c) the Ombudsman (ie the Parliamentary, Health Service or Local Government Commissioner)
(d) a Mental Health Review Tribunal
(e) a health or social services authority or Community Health Council
(f) the hospital managers
(g) any legally qualified person instructed by the patient
(h) the European Commission or Court of Human Rights.

ACCESS TO THE COURTS

A patient wishing to sue a person who has acted in accordance with the provisions of the Mental Health Act faces a complex procedural barrier. This applies, for example, in the case of a patient who wants to sue his doctor, a social worker or his nearest relative for making an application or recommendation for compulsory admission.

The patient needs permission to sue, and he will not be granted this permission unless he can show reasonable grounds for the contention that the person he wishes to sue acted in bad faith or without reasonable care. It does not matter whether or not the person actually had jurisdiction to act: he may have been acting unlawfully, but he has the full protection of the law as long as he undertook what he believed to be his legitimate duties under the Mental Health Act in good faith and with reasonable care. Permission to initiate *civil* proceedings must be given by the High Court; permission in respect of *criminal* proceedings must be granted by the Director of Public Prosecutions (s139).

The scope of section 139 is illustrated by Ashingdane's case (Court of Appeal, 18 February 1980) in which a patient's transfer from Broadmoor to Oakwood Hospital was blocked because two branches of the Confederation of Health Service Employees (COHSE) were operating a ban on restricted patients. Ashingdane instituted High Court proceedings against the Secretary of State, the Kent Area Health Authority and COHSE, but the High Court stayed the proceedings since permission had not been sought under section 141 of the 1959 Act (now section 139). The Court of Appeal dismissed an appeal by the patient in respect of the Secretary of State and the AHA, but allowed his appeal in respect of COHSE.

The Ashingdane case has been held admissible by the European Commission of Human Rights, *inter alia,* under Article 6(1) of the Convention which guarantees a person the right to a fair trial in the determination of a civil right (application no 8225/78; admissibility decision given 5 February 1982). A decision on the merits of this case is now awaited, but it is expected that the Commission will decide that section 141 deprives a person of a substantive, not a procedural, right, which is outside the scope of Article 6(1)

The 1983 Act takes into account part of the criticism implicit in the decision on Ashingdane's case. Section 139 protects staff (as did section 141 in the 1959 Act), but there is no longer any barrier to stop a patient bringing a court action against the Secretary of State or a health authority.

INFORMAL PATIENTS

The Mental Health Act does not expressly exempt informal patients from the provisions relating to access to the courts; nonetheless, one court has ruled that section 141 of the 1959 Act (now section 139) does *not* apply to informal patients *(R v Runighian [1977]* Criminal Law Review 361). It would certainly not apply if a member of staff used wrongful force against an informal patient.

CHANGES FROM THE 1959 ACT

Section 141 of the 1959 Act was subject to extensive criticism because it deprived patients of the fundamental right of unrestricted access to the courts to redress their grievances. The provision was based upon the assumption that patients are excessively fond of litigation and would want to bring unwarranted court actions against staff. However, the great majority of patients is withdrawn, isolated and vulnerable, and needs encouragement to secure even the most genuine of legal rights.

The 1983 Act does not state expressly that section 139 does not apply to informal patients (as the 1978 White Paper proposed it should). It does, however, change the terms of the patient's burden of proof from *substantial* to *reasonable* grounds; it requires that consent for *criminal* proceedings must be given by the Director of Public Prosecutions rather than the High Court; and it excludes the Secretary of State and health authorities from the protection of section 139. It is worth pointing out that social services authorities continue to enjoy the protection of section 139 as long as they are acting in accordance with the provisions of the Act.

VOTING RIGHTS

A number of changes concerning patients' right to vote was introduced in the Mental Health (Amendment) Act 1982. The law relating to the right of in-patients in mental illness and mental handicap hospitals to vote is consolidated in section 7 of the Representation of the People Act 1983: this came into effect on 1 April 1983. Regulations have been issued in accordance with section 53 of the Representation of the People Act 1983, and a circular has been issued to health authorities. The law enables certain longer-stay patients to make a *patient's declaration* which will entitle them to have their names entered on the electoral register in respect of an address outside the hospital.

BACKGROUND

A person is entitled to vote if he is entered on the electoral register as a resident of a particular locality. Section 4(3) of the Representation of the People Act 1949 prevented a patient 'in any establishment maintained wholly or mainly for the reception and treatment of persons suffering from mental disorder' from using the hospital as a place of residence for voting purposes. This created a number of anomalies; for example, an informal patient who had a home address could be registered at that address, and could visit a polling station or be treated as an absentee voter. Equally anomalous, a patient in a psychiatric wing of a district general hospital could use that hospital as a place of residence for voting purposes.

*Two cases brought by MIND established the principle that if a resident of a mental illness or mental handicap hospital was not mentally disordered within the meaning of the Mental Health Act, he *could* use the hospital as a place of residence for voting purposes. The DHSS and the Home Office issued circulars following each case giving guidance to hospitals and registration officers (RPA 261; HN(76) 180). Thus, residents who are not mentally disordered, and who are in hospital only because they have no home, are *not* considered to be *patients*. They are therefore entitled to use the hospital as a place of residence for voting purposes.

Detained patients cannot be entered on the electoral register in any circumstances.

***Winwick Hospital:** *Wild and Others v The Electoral Registration Officer for the Borough of Warrington.* Judgement given in Warrington County Court on 15 June 1976.

Calderstones Hospital: *Smith and Others v Jackson (Electoral Registration Officer for Clitheroe).* Heard at Blackburn County Court on 16 September 1981.

SCOPE AND DEFINITIONS

The provisions of the Representation of the People Act 1983 apply only to patients in establishments 'maintained wholly or mainly for the reception and treatment of persons suffering from mental disorder'. These include mental illness and mental handicap hospitals and private mental nursing homes, but not hostels where residents are not given treatment. The definition also excludes psychiatric wards of general hospitals, and old people's homes. Just as in the 1949 legislation, residents in general hospitals, nursing homes, hostels etc can be registered at the address of the home or institution where they live, and are entitled to be included on the electoral register in the usual way. In addition, people who live in mental illness or mental handicap hospitals but who have a home outside the hospital can still be registered at that home address. Householders will continue to be advised to include on the electoral registration form the names of any informal patients who are usually resident at their address, but temporarily away. Such informal patients can vote as before, and can take advantage of absent voter facilities, if appropriate.

NOTIFICATION TO PATIENTS

Health authorities (ie the hospital managers) must now give informal patients who will not be registered at their home address notice that they are entitled to make a patient's declaration for voting purposes.

Patient's declaration

The patient must declare *without assistance* that he is an informal mental patient, and must give the United Kingdom address where he would be resident if he were not a mental patient. If a patient cannot give such an address, any UK address (other than a mental hospital) at which he has resided is acceptable.

These provisions are designed to ensure that all patients who wish to make a declaration can supply an address, but they offer a considerble degree of scope. The address where the patient would be resident if he were not in hospital might be his family home or that of a relative or friend. If he cannot provide an address where he would otherwise be resident, he can declare any UK address at which he has ever lived, for example a private home, a hostel or an orphanage. The fact that a former address no longer exists because of redevelopment etc does not prevent it from being given in a declaration.

The declaration must be made annually, on or before the qualifying date, and the appropriate forms are available from Her Majesty's Stationery Office (HMSO).

The provision that the declaration be made *without assistance* does not apply to help required because the patient is blind or has a physical disability. The only requirement is that the patient must be able to understand the information requested on the form and to communicate it to the person responsible for attesting the declaration. He can be given help with reading and writing, and with enquiries about previous addresses.

The health authority must appoint a member of the hospital staff to attest patients' declarations: this simply involves the member of staff verifying that, to the best of his knowledge, the declaration is correct.

The completion of a declaration gives a patient the right to be entered on the electoral register, and to vote in person or by post.

CHANGES FROM THE REPRESENTATION OF THE PEOPLE ACT 1949

The new arrangements in respect of the electoral registration of informal mental patients introduce new principles into electoral law. First, the provision that the declaration must be completed without assistance appears to represent an implicit *capacity test;* this is apart from the common law tests of capacity to vote which apply to all voters. In practice, social workers sometimes help people living in the community to complete electoral registration forms. Second, the new arrangements are still anomalous in that a mental hospital cannot be given as a place of residence for voting purposes, while other kinds of hospital can. This provision was intended to prevent mental patients from influencing the outcome of elections in the constituency where the hospital is located; however, this cannot be considered a sound policy since it perpetuates the discrimination against mentally disordered people who wish to exercise their right to vote in the area where they live.

CHAPTER 10

THE ROLE OF THE HOSPITAL MANAGERS

The hospital managers (defined on p 5) have a variety of important mandatory duties to fulfil under current mental health legislation. Their legal responsibilities and the practical problems they are likely to face in implementing them are discussed in this chapter.

ADMISSION

(i) **Availability of beds:** in practice consultants (who are employed by the Regional Health Authority) make beds available, but the managers should keep under review all admissions to hospitals for which they are responsible. The Secretary of State for Social Services, as manager of the special hospitals, has a particular obligation to provide beds in the special hospitals, and must ensure that the statutory criteria under section 4 of the National Health Service Act 1977 (see chapter 1) are satisfied.

(ii) **Part II admissions:** an application for admission under Part II is sufficient authority for the managers to detain a patient in the hospital in accordance with the provisions of the Act (s6(2)).

(iii) **Part III admissions:** a hospital order gives the managers sufficient authority to detain a patient in accordance with the provisions of the Act (s40(1)).

(iv) **Rectification of defective applications and recommendations** (s15).

These legal requirements give hospital managers the specific responsibility to act as the detaining authority in accordance with the provisions of the Mental Health Act. It is absolutely clear that the managers are ultimately accountable for the lawfulness of each patient's detention. In order to be certain that they are acting lawfully, managers should scrutinise all applications and recommendations relating to compulsory admission.

Some patients or their representatives may wish to have access to applications or recommendations to ensure that a compulsory admission was lawful. In the past some managers, but not all, have been prepared to release the documents. Certainly, if the documentation is not in order the patient has the legal remedy of *habeas corpus,* and a court could require that the relevant documents be released.

One of the responsibilities of the MHAC is to ensure that all compulsory admissions are lawful. It is likely that the Commission will not examine all the documents itself, but will endeavour to make sure that the managers carry out their duties efficiently.

DETENTION AND RENEWAL

(i) The managers are authorised to detain any patient in accordance with the provisions of the Act.

(ii) The managers receive the RMO's report renewing the authority to detain; when such a report is received the managers must, unless they decide to discharge the patient, inform him that the authority for his detention has been renewed (s20).

(iii) The managers may discharge unrestricted patients (s23).

(iv) The managers receive discharge orders from the nearest relative and barring certificates from the RMO (s25) (see p 29).

The authority to detain a patient will lapse if it is not renewed. The managers must ensure that the RMO follows the correct procedures for renewal, and must also notify the patient that his detention has been renewed. The patient can apply to a MHRT during each period of renewal.

The managers have the specific right to discharge unrestricted patients. This is an independent safeguard, and is quite separate from the power MHRTs and the RMO have to order a discharge. The managers can discharge a patient against medical advice if they feel that it is appropriate.

Thus, the managers have the power of discharge, but the Act does not specify any particular steps they must take to fulfil their responsibilities. However, the managers should certainly visit the hospitals they cover, and should make sure that they are generally familiar with the patients and staff. When a request for discharge is made, the managers should read the RMO's report and any other reports or evidence put forward by the patient. Having considered these reports, they must decide whether there is reasonable justification for the patient's continued detention. They may find it helpful to hold a managers' hearing to give the patient the opportunity to speak to them in person, and to marshall his evidence. There is a particularly strong case for a managers' hearing when the patient has missed his chance to apply to a MHRT: a patient is also entitled to request such a hearing.

Managers should also be kept informed of general trends in each hospital, and should be able to monitor the use of certain powers, for example compulsory admission in cases of emergency. It may be that there has been excessive use of certain powers, in which case the managers should investigate in order to assure themselves that the hospital has been using these powers legitimately.

REFERENCE TO MENTAL HEALTH REVIEW TRIBUNALS

The 1983 Act imposes on the managers a new duty to refer patients to a MHRT (see chapter 6).

CORRESPONDENCE

The managers have to take certain decisions about withholding correspondence sent by, or to, detained patients (see pp 60-61).

INFORMATION FOR PATIENTS AND NEAREST RELATIVES

The Mental Health Act specifically requires the hospital managers to give certain information to patients (s132). The managers must take 'such steps as are practicable' to ensure that a detained patient understands—

- the provisions under which he is detained and his right to apply to a Mental Health Review Tribunal;
- his right to be discharged by the RMO, the managers and, if applicable, his nearest relative;
- his rights in respect of consent to treatment under Part IV of the Act;
- the functions of the MHAC and its role in protecting detained patients;
- the correspondence provisions and the code of practice.

A patient must be given this information both orally and in writing as soon as practicable after the commencement of his detention. The managers must also supply the nearest relative with a copy of the written information given to the patient.

When a detained patient is to be discharged other than by the nearest relative, the managers must, if practicable, inform the person who appears to be his nearest relative within seven days before the discharge. However, the patient or the nearest relative is entitled to request that no such information should be conveyed.

GENERAL MANAGEMENT FUNCTIONS

In addition to the duties specified under the Act, the managers should also undertake the usual functions of health service managers such as investigating complaints (this is already contemplated in s120(1)(b)), and reviewing the way hospitals provide or help the patient gain access to services, welfare benefits and pocket money. Thus, these managerial functions are important in respect of specific statutory objectives, and they may also have broader implications for service development, management and patient care.

In the past, the managers' responsibilities have often been delegated to unit administrators and, in turn, to designated ward staff, and it is crucial that managers have confidence in the staff to whom their powers are delegated. This is not to suggest that delegation is not proper; it may, for example, be useful to delegate to a ward nurse or ASW the duty to give a detained patient specific information. However, the managers must ensure that the responsibilities for which they are legally accountable are being discharged lawfully, efficiently and caringly.

Many of the functions of the managers will be subject to review by the Mental Health Act Commission.

CHAPTER 11

THE MANAGEMENT OF PATIENTS' PROPERTY & AFFAIRS

BACKGROUND

Prior to the passage of the Mental Health Act 1959, patients who were compulsorily detained were presumed incompetent to manage their financial affairs; there was no specific enquiry into their medical condition or capacity for rational understanding.

The 1957 Royal Commission on the Law relating to Mental Illness and Mental Deficiency observed that a patient's legal status could not in itself indicate whether or not he was capable of handling his own affairs. Indeed, the Commission accepted that unsoundness of mind was not necessarily a completely disabling condition. It concluded that 'the law and administrative arrangements dealing with patients' property should not be in any way dependent on whether the patient is in hospital or not, or whether a hospital patient has been admitted with or without compulsion': each individual case should be decided on the basis of an objective test of mental capacity. These recommendations were incorporated into section 101 of the 1959 Act in relation to the jurisdiction of the Court of Protection. The Mental Health (Amendment) Act 1982 made no changes to the powers of the Court, and the functions of the Court of Protection are set out in Part VII of the Mental Health Act 1983. Its procedures are governed by the Court of Protection Rules, SI 1982, no 322. These Rules are currently under review.

The Court's powers and responsibilities are summarised in this chapter. For a detailed account and policy analysis see the MIND special report **The Court of Protection**.

THE JURISDICTION OF THE COURT

Statutory authority: s94(2)

Maximum duration of detention: until revoked

Criterion: 'a person is incapable, by reason of mental disorder, of managing and administering his property and affairs'

Procedure: one medical recommendation

Effect: Court can manage and control a patient's property and affairs; it has the option of appointing a receiver

A person under the jurisdiction of the Court is termed a *patient,* irrespective of whether or not he is in hospital or is liable to be detained. It is important to observe that a person under the Court's jurisdiction need not be suffering from one of the four specific categories of mental disorder. Furthermore, the medical evidence required can come from a single doctor with no special experience of mental disorder; in practice the medical recommendation is often given by the patient's GP. Once a person is deemed mentally incapable of managing his own affairs, he cannot give a power of attorney or any other authority appointing a person of his choice to manage his property; any such authority given prior to his incapacity may be considered invalid.

EXERCISE OF JURISDICTION AND PROCEDURES

The Court exercises its jurisdiction through three main procedures: receivership; a shortened and less complex procedure generally reserved for cases where property and assets do not exceed £5,000; and emergency powers. The usual course of action is to appoint a receiver to handle the patient's income and administer his property under the direction of the Court: the receiver may be a relative, the director of a local authority social services department or, exceptionally, the Official Solicitor. The Court charges costs and fees on a fixed scale, and these are debited to the patient's estate.

The Court of Protection is both an office of the Lord Chancellor's Department, and a judicial body. Patients who are unhappy with a judicial decision taken by the Court can appeal to the High Court, and hardship caused by maladministration may be investigated by the Parliamentary Commissioner for Administration.

For further information write to the Court of Protection at 25 Store Street, London WC1.

THE LORD CHANCELLOR'S VISITORS

The Lord Chancellor appoints Visitors who make personal contact with patients in accordance with the directions of the Court of Protection. They investigate matters relating to patients' ability to manage property and affairs and any other issues which fall within the jurisdiction of the Court.

The Supreme Court Act 1981, which came into force in January 1982, introduced the provision that the Visitors' Panel should consist of Medical, Legal and General Visitors. General Visitors are civil servants employed in the Lord Chancellor's Department.

CHAPTER 12
REMOVAL OF PATIENTS WITHIN THE UNITED KINGDOM ETC

Part VI of the Act gives the Home Secretary the power to remove and return certain patients within the United Kingdom: this applies to the removal of patients to Scotland (s80); the removal of patients to and from Northern Ireland (ss81, 82); and the removal of patients to and from the Channel Islands and the Isle of Man (ss83-85). Part VI also makes provision for the return of patients who are absent without leave from hospitals in Northern Ireland (s87), England and Wales (s88), or the Channel Islands or the Isle of Man (s89).

In general, these powers can only be exercised in the case of a patient who is liable to be detained (except for remand or on an interim hospital order), or subject to guardianship. The Home Secretary must be satisfied that appropriate arrangements have been made to admit the patient to hospital or to receive him into guardianship in the place to which he is to be removed.

REMOVAL OF ALIENS

In addition to his powers to remove and return patients within the United Kingdom, the Home Secretary can also remove alien patients to a country outside the United Kingdom (s86). This provision applies to any patient who is neither a British nor a Commonwealth citizen with the right to live in the United Kingdom under section 2(1)(b) of the Immigration Act 1971. The patient must be receiving treatment for *mental illness (not* any of the other forms of mental disorder); he must be an *in-patient* (not on a leave of absence); and he must actually be *detained* (not simply *liable* to be detained) under the Act other than on remand for report or treatment, or on an interim hospital order.

The Home Secretary must be satisfied that proper arrangements have been made for the patient's removal to a country outside the United Kingdom and for his care and treatment there, and that such a removal is in the patient's interests. He can only exercise his powers if he has the approval of a Mental Health Review Tribunal.

CHAPTER 13
RIGHTS IN THE COMMUNITY

The Royal Commission on the Law relating to Mental Illness and Mental Deficiency adopted the fundamental philosophy that, wherever possible, care should be provided in a community setting without the use of compulsion. The provision of treatment, care and support for mentally disordered people living in the community is the joint responsibility of health and social services authorities in co-operation with the voluntary sector. The legislation which allows, and often requires, authorities to establish community services is described in this chapter. For a much more detailed account see Gostin, **Mental Health Services and the Law,** 5th edition (Shaw & Sons, 1984).

HEALTH SERVICES

Section 1 of the National Health Service Act 1977 imposes upon the Secretary of State for Social Services the duty to promote a comprehensive health service designed to secure improvement in the physical and mental health of people in England and Wales. To such extent as he considers necessary 'to meet all reasonable requirements', the Secretary of State must provide facilities for the prevention of illness and for the care and after-care of people who have suffered, or are suffering, from physical or mental illness (National Health Service Act 1977, s3). These powers and duties are delegated by the Secretary of State to Regional Health Authorities, and by them to District Health Authorities.

SOCIAL SERVICES

With the Secretary of State's approval a local social services authority *may,* and, to such extent as he may direct, *shall* make arrangements for the prevention of illness and for the care and after-care of people who have suffered, or are suffering, from physical or mental illness (National Health Service Act 1977, s21, sch 8, para 2). The Secretary of State has issued directions which impose upon social services departments a mandatory duty to provide prevention, care and after-care services (see local authority circular 19/74).

AFTER-CARE SERVICES

Section 117 of the Mental Health Act 1983 lays a duty to provide after-care services on the District Health Authority and local social services authority, in co-operation with relevant voluntary agencies. This provision applies to patients who have been detained for treatment (s3), under a hospital order (s37) or under a transfer direction (ss47, 48) and are then discharged.

After-care services, which are not defined, must be provided until the District Health Authority and social services authority are satisfied that the person no longer needs such services. The authority which has the mandatory duty under this section is the one with responsibility for the area where the person concerned is resident or is sent upon discharge.

During the Parliamentary debates on after-care, the Government suggested that the provisions of section 117 duplicate a power which health and social services authorities already enjoy. This is partly true. However, section 117 expressly locates the duty to provide after-care within the primary piece of mental health legislation; it states specifically which authority has the mandatory duty; and it requires that the duty stays in force until a person no longer has a need for after-care services. This is therefore a very important provision which should benefit detained patients who may need a home, occupation, support or continued medical and/or nursing care and attention after their discharge.

It would have been far preferable had the Act imposed a duty to provide after-care for *all* patients, detained or not. The Act should also have made clear what services are required: the term *after-care* is left undefined. Local authority circular 19/74 outlines the kind of after-care services which should reasonably be provided.

HOUSING SERVICES

Department of Health and Social Security statistics on reasons for admission to hospital show that substantial numbers of people are admitted primarily on domiciliary and social grounds. Having been admitted, they may remain in hospital for prolonged periods while suitable accommodation is sought. In such cases the institution has a distinct *hotel* or *asylum* function in providing lodgings for vulnerable people who are homeless.

ACCOMMODATION PROVIDED BY SOCIAL SERVICES DEPARTMENTS: THE SPECIAL NEED PROVISION

Local social services departments have the power and a general responsibility to provide special residential accommodation for mentally disordered people who usually live in their areas: this includes patients who were living in the area immediately prior to hospital admission. Residential homes, hostels, group homes, minimum support facilities and other appropriate accommodation should be provided in this way.

ACCOMMODATION PROVIDED BY HOUSING DEPARTMENTS: THE GENERAL NEED PROVISION

Local housing departments have a general responsibility to review the needs of people in their area and to develop housing schemes to meet those needs. They are authorised to provide a range of accommodation which would be suitable for mentally disordered people, including single dwellings, lodgings, group homes, bedsits, sheltered housing and hostels.

The Housing (Homeless Persons) Act 1977 is potentially a very important statute for mentally disordered people. Section 4 of that Act imposes upon housing departments a mandatory duty to provide accommodation for people who are homeless or threatened with homelessness if they have a priority need. Section 1 states that a person is homeless if he has no accommodation which he, together with others who normally live with him, is entitled to occupy. It is specifically stated in section 2 that a homeless person or a person threatened with homelessness has a priority need for accommodation if he, or any person who lives or might reasonably be expected to live with him, is 'vulnerable as a result of mental illness or handicap or other special reason'.

Thus, a mentally ill or mentally handicapped person who is in hospital only because he has no suitable accommodation, or a compulsorily detained patient who is about to be discharged and has no home, should be provided with accommodation by the housing department. This is a clear mandatory duty which should be enforced on behalf of mentally ill or mentally handicapped people (and their families) if they are homeless or threatened with homelessness.

CONCLUSION

One of the great unrealised objectives of the Royal Commission on the Law relating to Mental Illness and Mental Deficiency, which sat between 1954 and 1959, was to effect a massive shift of resources from hospital care to care in the community. The Commission's report proclaimed that 'the recommendations of our witnesses were generally in favour of a shift in emphasis from hospital care to community care. In relation to almost all forms of mental disorder, there is increasing medical emphasis on forms of treatment and training and social services which can be given without bringing patients into hospital as in-patients or which make it possible to discharge them from hospital sooner than was usual in the past'. In the light of these recommendations, the Commission advocated 'a general re-orientation away from institutional care in its present form and towards community care'. This would result, the report confirmed, in the expansion of local authority services including 'provision of residential accommodation . . . adequate training facilities . . . occupational or training centres, sheltered workshops and social centres'.

And yet, in one of the debates during the passage of the Mental Health (Amendment) Act 1982 through the House of Lords, Lord Elton, then Parliamentary Under-Secretary of State at the Department of Health and Social Security, admitted that there were only 3,724 places for mentally ill people in local authority homes and hostels. The DHSS statistics for local authority personal social services at 31 March 1982 in fact reveal that there were 4,063 such places – this figure is not even twice that recorded in 1974. The number of places for mentally handicapped people is better at 13,144, although this is little more than double the 1974 provision. Despite the exhortations of the Commission 26 years ago, there are still 17 local authorities in England and Wales which provide *no* residential places for mentally ill people, relying on voluntary effort alone; indeed there appear to be two authorities with no residential accommodation of any sort at all in their areas. Concurrent with this failure to develop community resources, there have been other changes. Most patients, including detained patients, stay in hospital for shorter lengths of time and the number of in-patients has fallen. This change does not hide, however, the failure to provide *real* alternatives to hospital-centred care. Whatever the legal efficacy of section 117 (the after-care clause) of the 1983 Mental Health Act, it does represent a significant statement of the legislature's discontent with the provision of care for detained patients after their discharge; this was clearly evident from the Parliamentary debates in both Houses.

The underlying principle of the 1983 Mental Health Act is that of the *least restrictive alternative.* Every professional involved in the operation of the new Act is enjoined to ensure that compulsory admission to hospital is the last resort and that *no* other alternative is feasible. If this laudable aim is to be achieved, not only must the law establish it as a duty, but those burdened with that duty must have real alternatives available to them. In the main, the new Act applies to that tiny percentage of mentally ill and mentally handicapped people who are compulsorily detained. It must be the hope and objective of all those involved in the treatment and care of mentally disordered people, be they patients themselves, doctors, nurses, social workers, psychologists or other mental health professionals, that the full potential of the Act is realised, not only for detained patients but for informal patients as well.

SELECTED BIBLIOGRAPHY

LEGISLATION AND STATUTORY INSTRUMENTS

The Health and Social Services and Social Security Adjudications Act 1983
The Mental Health Act 1983
The Mental Health Act Commission (Establishment and Constitution) Order 1983
The Mental Health Act Commission Regulations 1983
The Mental Health (Hospital, Guardianship and Consent to Treatment) Regulations 1983
The Mental Health Review Tribunal Rules of Procedure 1983
The National Health Service Act 1977

GOVERNMENT DOCUMENTS AND REPORTS

Committee on Mentally Abnormal Offenders (Lord Butler), Cmnd 6244. (1975) London, HMSO.
Mental Health Act 1983 Explanatory Memorandum (1983) London, DHSS.
Reform of Mental Health Legislation, Cmnd 8405. (1981) London, HMSO.
Review of the Mental Health Act 1959. (1976) London, HMSO.
Review of the Mental Health Act 1959, Cmnd 7320. (1978) London, HMSO.
Royal Commission on the Law Relating to Mental Illness and Mental Deficiency (Lord Percy) 1954-1957, Cmnd 189. (1957) London, HMSO.

BOOKS

BLUGLASS, R. (1983) *A Guide to the Mental Health Act.* London, Heinemann.
GOSTIN, L. (1983) *The Court of Protection.* London, MIND.
GOSTIN, L. (1975, 1977) *A Human Condition,* two volumes. London, MIND.
GOSTIN, L. (1984) *Mental Health Services and the Law,* 5th edition. London, Shaw & Sons.
GOSTIN, L., RASSABY, E. & BUCHAN, A. (in press) *Mental Health Review Tribunals.* London, Oyez Longman.
HOGGETT, B. (in press) *Social Work and Law: Mental Health,* 2nd edition. London, Sweet & Maxwell.
KINAHAN, A. (1983) *Mental Health Act 1983: Current Law Statutes Reprints.* London, Sweet & Maxwell.
MIND (1983) *The Mental Health Case Law Review.* London, MIND.
MIND (1981) *The Mental Health Year Book 1981/82.* London, MIND.
OLSEN, R., MEACHER, M. & GOSTIN, L. (1983) *A Guide to the Mental Health Act.* Birmingham, BASW.

TAYLOR, E.R. (1978) *Heywood and Massey: Court of Protection Practice.* London, Stevens & Sons.

VENABLES, H.D. (1975) *A Guide to the Law Affecting Mental Patients.* London, Butterworths.

WHITEHEAD, T. (1982) *Mental Illness and the Law.* Oxford, Blackwells.

CHAPTER

GOSTIN, L. (1983) *The ideology of entitlement: the contemporary application of law to psychiatry.* In P. BEAN (ed). *Mental Illness: Changes and Trends.* London, John Wiley & Sons.

ARTICLES

GOSTIN, L. (1982) *Human rights, judicial review and the mentally disordered offender.* Criminal Law Review 779.

GOSTIN, L. (in press) *Contemporary historical approaches to mental health legislation. Journal of Law & Society.*

APPENDIX I
GLOSSARY OF TERMS

Hospital   Defined in section 145. (See chapter 1, p 4).

Hospital order   An order made by a criminal court under section 37 directing that an offender be detained in a specified hospital.

Informal admission   Arranged under section 131. (See chapter 1, pp 5-6).

Managers   Defined in section 145. (See chapter 1, p 5).

Medical treatment   Defined in section 145. (See chapter 1, p 4).

Mental Health Act 1983, Part II   Part II of the Act is concerned with civil admission to hospital (ie detention justified in the interests of a mentally disordered patient's health or safety, not because the patient has committed a criminal offence).

Mental Health Act 1983, Part III   Part III of the Act is concerned with patients involved in criminal proceedings. Admission to hospital under Part III means that the patient is detained directly as a result of appearing before a criminal court.

Mental Health Act 1983, Part IV   Part IV is concerned with consent to treatment. A patient to whom Part IV does not apply has the same right to withhold consent to treatment as any other National Health Service patient.

Mental Health Act Commission (MHAC)   A special health authority established by the Secretary of State under the National Health Service Act 1977, section 11. Section 121 of the Mental Health Act further directs the Secretary of State to delegate certain of his responsibilities conferred under the Mental Health Act to the MHAC. (See chapter 8.)

Mental Health Review Tribunal (MHRT)   MHRTs are independent bodies which have their statutory basis in Part V of the Mental Health Act 1983. Tribunal procedure is governed by the Mental Health Review Tribunal Rules of Procedure 1983. It is possible to appeal to the High Court against a MHRT decision on points of law by means of a case-stated procedure. (See chapter 6.)

Patient   Defined in section 145. (See chapter 1, p 4).

Responsible medical officer (RMO)   The medical practitioner in charge of the treatment of a detained patient. (Technically it is possible for the RMO to have charge of an informal patient receiving treatment under section 57.) He has specific duties including the renewal of detention (s20), and the power to grant trial leave of absence (s17). Hospital patients are generally under the clinical charge of a consultant.

Restriction direction   A transfer direction with restrictions on discharge imposed by the Home Secretary in accordance with section 49. The restrictions continue in force until the date on which the person would have been entitled to be released from prison with remission (ie the earliest date of release). When the restrictions lapse the person may continue to be detained in hospital under a transfer direction.

Restriction order An order under section 41 imposed by a superior court in addition to a hospital order. When a restriction order is made, the Home Secretary must give his consent to decisions which would usually be taken by the RMO or the hospital managers, for example in respect of leave of absence, transfer or discharge. A restriction order may be imposed for a fixed period, but is generally made without limit of time.

Restricted patient A patient who is subject to a restriction order.

Special hospital Defined in section 145. (See chapter 1, p 5).

Transfer direction An order made by the Home Secretary under section 47 directing that a person serving a sentence of imprisonment be transferred to a hospital. On the expiry date of the prison sentence, the patient may continue to be detained under a hospital order.

APPENDIX II:
TABLES

ADMISSION TO HOSPITAL: PART II

Legislation	Criteria	Application	Medical recommendations	Effect
A Admission for assessment Mental Health Act 1983, section 2	(a) mental disorder which warrants detention in hospital for assessment (or assessment followed by medical treatment) **and** (b) patient ought to be detained in the interests of his own health or safety or for the protection of others	(i) *nearest relative*, in which case hospital managers must inform local social services authority so that a report on the patient's social circumstances can be provided **or** (ii) *approved social worker* who must interview the patient and satisfy himself that detention in hospital is the most appropriate way of providing care and medical treatment, given all the circumstances of the case	Two doctors, one of whom must be approved under section 12. Patient to be examined by both doctors either together or separately within five days of one another. Doctors are not to be from the same hospital, subject to the exceptions in section 12(4) of the Act	Patient detained for 28 days maximum Patient can be treated without his consent in accordance with the provisions of Part IV of the Act
B Admission for treatment Mental Health Act 1983, section 3	Mental illness, severe mental impairment, psychopathic disorder or mental impairment of a nature or degree which makes medical treatment in hospital appropriate. In the case of psychopathic disorder or mental impairment, the treatment must be likely to alleviate or prevent a deterioration of the patient's condition	As for an admission for assessment (s2) but an ASW cannot make an application if the nearest relative objects	As for an admission for assessment (s2)	Patient detained for a maximum of six months; renewable for a further six months and then for periods of one year at a time

82

C Admission for assessment in an emergency Mental Health Act 1983, section 4	Admission for assessment required as a matter of urgent necessity	(i) *nearest relative* **or** (ii) *approved social worker* Patient must be seen by applicant during the 24 hours before the application is made	One written recommendation by any doctor, but if possible by a doctor with previous knowledge of the patient	Patient detained for a maximum of 72 hours unless second medical opinion is given and received by hospital managers within that period Provisions of Part IV on consent to treatment do not apply
D Patients already in hospital Mental Health Act 1983, section 5(2)	It appears to the doctor in charge of treatment of an informal patient that an application for compulsory detention 'ought to be made'	None	A report by the doctor in charge of the patient's treatment or by one deputy nominated by him for this purpose	Patient is detained for a maximum of 72 hours from the time of the report Provisions of Part IV on consent to treatment do not apply
E Nurse's holding power Mental Health Act 1983, section 5(4)	(a) an informal patient is suffering from mental disorder to such a degree that it is necessary for his health or safety or for the protection of others that he be immediately restrained from leaving hospital **and** (b) it is not practicable to secure the immediate attendance of the doctor in charge of treatment or his deputy (see under D)	None	None. Authority to detain is a report by a nurse of the prescribed class, ie first level mental illness or mental handicap nurse	Patient detained for a maximum of six hours from the time the report is made by the nurse or until the arrival of the doctor in charge of treatment or his nominated deputy, if this is earlier

continued overleaf

ADMISSSION TO HOSPITAL: PART II (continued)

Legislation	Criteria	Application	Medical recommendations	Effect
F Reception into guardianship Mental Health Act 1983, section 7	(a) mental illness, severe mental impairment, psychopathic disorder or mental impairment of a nature or degree which warrants reception into guardianship **and** (b) it is necessary in the interests of the welfare of the patient or for the protection of others **and** (c) the patient must be over 16 years old	(i) *nearest relative* **or** (ii) *approved social worker*	As for an admission for assessment (s2)	The person is received into the guardianship of the local social services authority or a named person who is acceptable to the authority The duration of a guardianship order is as for section 3 The guardian has the power to require— (a) the patient to reside at a specified place (b) the patient to attend at specified places and times for medical treatment, occupation, education or training (c) that access to the patient be given to any doctor, approved social worker or other specified person A patient received into guardianship is not subject to the provisions of Part IV of the Act relating to consent to treatment

ADMISSION TO HOSPITAL: PART III
PATIENTS CONCERNED IN CRIMINAL PROCEEDINGS

Legislation	Criteria and evidence	Decision-maker (and burden of proof)	Effect
A Mental disorder present at the time of the offence			
(i) Special verdict of not guilty by reason of insanity Criminal Procedure (insanity) Act 1964, section 2	M'Naghten Rules: the offender did not know the nature and quality of the act or did not know that it was wrong No formal requirements – generally two medical opinions	Jury (Defence raises evidence and bears the burden of proof to 'a balance of probabilities')	Hospital order made with restrictions and without limit of time (mandatory) See C(ii) below
(ii) Diminished responsibility which is a plea in mitigation of sentence Homicide Act 1957, section 2	The offender suffers from an abnormality of mind which impairs his mental responsibility	Jury As A(i) above	Reduces charge of murder to one of manslaughter, thus avoiding the mandatory life sentence and allowing court a wide range of disposals
B Mental disorder present at the time of the trial			
(i) Transfer direction before trial	The defendant must be suffering from mental illness or severe mental impairment which makes it appropriate for him to be detained in a hospital for medical treatment; he must be in urgent need of such treatment Two medical opinions	Home Secretary	Hospital order with restrictions and without limit of time (mandatory) See C(ii) below

continued overleaf

ADMISSION TO HOSPITAL: PART III
PATIENTS CONCERNED IN CRIMINAL PROCEEDINGS (continued)

Legislation	Criteria and evidence	Decision-maker (and burden of proof)	Effect
(ii) Unfit to plead Criminal Procedure (Insanity) Act 1964, section 4	The defendant is unable to understand the proceedings well enough to make a proper defence, to challenge a juror, and to comprehend the evidence	Jury (If the *defence* raises the issue, it bears the burden of proof to the balance of probabilities. If the *prosecution* raises the issue, it bears the burden, beyond a reasonable doubt)	The facts of the original charge are not examined if the issue of unfitness to plead is raised at the outset of the trial; if trial proceedings have already started, they are abandoned once the issue is raised
	As A(i) above, except that in some cases only one medical opinion is put before the court		The defendant must be detained in hospital, with restrictions on discharge imposed without limit of time – see C(ii) below. He may be remitted for trial at a later date
			Once he is detained, the patient can apply to a Mental Health Review Tribunal during the first six months of detention. If he does not exercise his right to apply to a MHRT, he will be automatically referred to a tribunal after the six months have expired

C Mental disorder present at the time of sentencing

	Crown Court or Magistrates' Court	
(i) Hospital order Mental Health Act 1983, section 37	The defendant is suffering from mental illness, psychopathic disorder, mental impairment or severe mental impairment which warrants his detention in a mental hospital. In the case of psychopathic disorder or mental impairment, such treatment must be likely to alleviate or prevent a deterioration of his condition	A hospital order has a similar effect to an admission for treatment under section 3 of the 1983 Act, ie detention is initially for a period of six months, and the order may be renewed for a further six months and then for periods of one year at a time.
	Two medical opinions are required. The court must be satisfied, on the written or oral evidence of the medical practitioner who would be in charge of the patient's treatment or some other person representing the hospital managers, that the criteria are fulfilled	The patient may be discharged at any time by the RMO, the hospital managers or a Mental Health Review Tribunal
	The Regional Health Authority must, at the request of the court provide information on available hospital facilities	

continued overleaf

ADMISSION TO HOSPITAL: PART III
PATIENTS CONCERNED IN CRIMINAL PROCEEDINGS (continued)

Legislation	Criteria and evidence	Decision-maker (and burden of proof)	Effect
(ii) Hospital order with restrictions on discharge, with or without limit of time Mental Health Act 1983, section 41	As C(i) above The court must also consider that restrictions on discharge are necessary to protect the public from serious harm	Crown Court	A restriction order may be made for a fixed period or without limit of time. Restricted patients cannot be discharged by RMO or hospital managers without the consent of the Home Secretary. However, a MHRT has the power to discharge a restricted patient
	Magistrates' Courts must remit defendant to a Crown Court in order for a restriction order to be made		
	The opinions of two medical practitioners are required, and one must give oral evidence to the court		The RMO must provide the Home Office with an annual report on the patient's progress
(iii) Probation order with a condition of psychiatric treatment Powers of Criminal Courts Act 1973, section 3	The condition of the defendant must be such that it requires and is susceptible to treatment, but does not warrant his detention in a hospital	Court	The patient must attend hospital for psychiatric treatment as an informal in-patient or on an out-patient basis
	The defendant must consent to the making of this order Two medical opinions are required		

D Mental disorder present after sentencing

(i) Transfer to hospital of a person serving sentence of imprisonment Mental Health Act 1983, section 47	As C(i) above, plus the Home Secretary must consider, having regard to the public interest, that the transfer of the prisoner to a mental hospital is expedient	Home Secretary	The prisoner is transferred from prison to hospital; an order made under section 47 has the same effect as a hospital order (s37)
(ii) Transfer from prison to hospital with restrictions on discharge Mental Health Act 1983, section 49	As C(ii) above	Home Secretary	As C(ii) above
			The patient may be returned to prison if the Home Secretary is notified by the RMO, any medical practitioner or a tribunal that he no longer requires treatment; or he may be released on licence if he would have been so released on return to prison
			The restrictions on discharge cease to have effect on what would have been the earliest date of release from prison. The patient is thereafter liable to be detained under the provisions described in D(i) above

E New provisions in the Mental Health Act 1983

(i) Remand to hospital for report on accused's mental condition Mental Health Act 1983, section 35	The defendant is suffering from mental illness, psychopathic disorder, mental impairment or severe mental impairment, and it would be impracticable for a report on his mental condition to be made if he were remanded on bail	Court	Duration of remand is no more than 28 days at a time or 12 weeks in all
	Opinion of one medical practitioner required		Person remanded in hospital for a medical report cannot be given treatment without his consent

continued overleaf

ADMISSION TO HOSPITAL: PART III PATIENTS CONCERNED IN CRIMINAL PROCEEDINGS (continued)

Legislation	Criteria and evidence	Decision-maker (and burden of proof)	Effect
(ii) Remand of accused person to hospital for treatment Mental Health Act 1983, section 36	The accused person is suffering from mental illness or severe mental impairment of a nature or degree which makes it appropriate for him to be detained in hospital Opinion of two medical practitioners required	Court	Duration of remand as in E(ii) above. However, the person *can* be treated without consent in certain circumstances in accordance with the provisions of Part IV of the Mental Health Act
(iii) Interim hospital order Mental Health Act 1983, section 38	The offender is suffering from mental illness, severe mental impairment psychopathic disorder or mental impairment, and there is reason to that the mental disorder is such that a hospital order may be apppropriate. Thus the person can be admitted on an interim hospital order to assess the suitability of hospital treatment Opinion of two medical practitioners required	Court	The detention is for a period not exceeding 12 weeks and may be continued for further periods of no more than 28 days at a time up to a maximum of six months in total

DECISIONS INVOLVING CONSENT TO TREATMENT

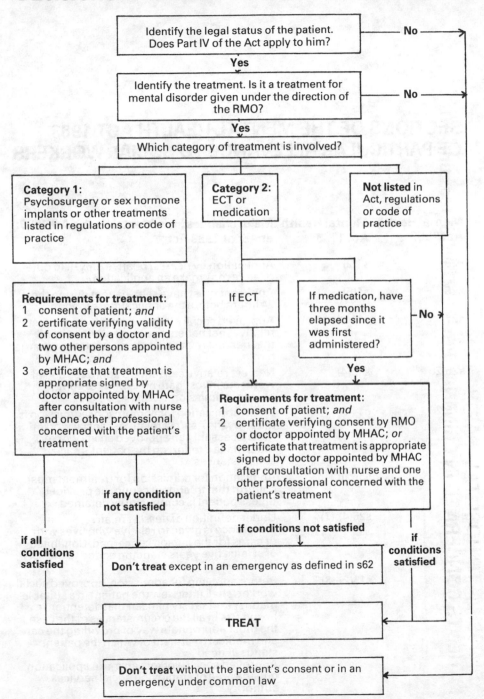

Identify the legal status of the patient. Does Part IV of the Act apply to him? — No →

Yes ↓

Identify the treatment. Is it a treatment for mental disorder given under the direction of the RMO? — No →

Yes ↓

Which category of treatment is involved?

Category 1: Psychosurgery or sex hormone implants or other treatments listed in regulations or code of practice

Category 2: ECT or medication

Not listed in Act, regulations or code of practice

Requirements for treatment:
1 consent of patient; *and*
2 certificate verifying validity of consent by a doctor and two other persons appointed by MHAC; *and*
3 certificate that treatment is appropriate signed by doctor appointed by MHAC after consultation with nurse and one other professional concerned with the patient's treatment

If ECT

If medication, have three months elapsed since it was first administered? — No →

Yes ↓

Requirements for treatment:
1 consent of patient; *and*
2 certificate verifying consent by RMO or doctor appointed by MHAC; *or*
3 certificate that treatment is appropriate signed by doctor appointed by MHAC after consultation with nurse and one other professional concerned with the patient's treatment

if any condition not satisfied

if conditions not satisfied

if all conditions satisfied

if conditions satisfied

Don't treat except in an emergency as defined in s62

TREAT

Don't treat without the patient's consent or in an emergency under common law

SECTIONS OF THE MENTAL HEALTH ACT 1983
OF PARTICULAR RELEVANCE TO SOCIAL WORKERS

Mental Health Act 1959	Mental Health Act 1983	Major changes from Mental Health Act 1959: effect of 1983 Act
s29	s4(2)	Application by *nearest* relative only. (No other relative may make an application)
s29	s4(5)	Applicant must have seen patient during the 24 hours before the application is made
s27	s11(3)	Approved social worker must inform nearest relative that patient has been admitted, and that nearest relative has the power to discharge him
s25/26	s13(4)	Nearest relative can require approved social worker to investigate possibility of compulsory admission
s25/26	s14	When application for compulsory admission is made by the nearest relative, a social worker (not necessarily an approved social worker) must make a report on the patient's social circumstances
s26	s3(2)(c)	Application for admission for treatment must confirm that treatment cannot be provided unless patient is compulsorily detained
s49	s26(4),(7)	Under definition of *nearest* relative, preference is given to relative who lives with or cares for the person concerned. Cohabitee of at least five years standing added to the list of relatives
s54	s13(2),(3)	Before applying for admission, approved social worker 'shall interview the patient in a suitable manner and satisfy himself that detention in a hospital is in all the circumstances of the case the most appropriate way of providing the care and medical treatment of which the patient stands in need' Approved social worker can make application outside area of employing social services authority

Mental Health Act 1959	Mental Health Act 1983	Major changes from Mental Health Act 1959: effect of 1983 Act
s34	s8	A guardian's powers used to be very wide-ranging. These have now been limited to essential powers to (a) specify residence; (b) specify attendance for treatment, occupation, education or training; (c) require access to patient to be given to doctor, approved social worker or other specified person. (Local social services authorities usually act as guardian)
—	s132	Hospital managers to take all practicable steps to inform detained patients of effect of section they are detained under, their right to apply to a MHRT, and also rights re (a) discharge (s25); (b) consent to treatment (Part IV); (c) code of practice (s118); (d) duty of Mental Health Act Commission to protect patients (s120); (e) post (s134)
—	s114	Two years after the passage of the Amendment Act (ie 28 October 1984), the responsibilities of mental welfare officers transferred to approved social workers. The local authority must appoint a 'sufficient number' of approved social workers to carry out the functions conferred by the 1983 Act. No-one can be appointed an approved social worker unless approved by the authority 'as having appropriate competence in dealing with persons who are suffering from mental disorder' Secretary of State lays down regulations specifying conditions of approval (eg CCETSW to set examinations)
—	s117	District Health Authorities and social services authorities in co-operation with voluntary organisations to provide after-care for those discharged from section 3 and section 37 orders

SUMMARY OF STATUTORY DUTIES AND FUNCTIONS OF SOCIAL WORKERS AND SOCIAL SERVICES AUTHORITIES

Duty or function and statutory authority	Description
Appointment of ASWs (s114)	ASW must be approved by his employing authority as having appropriate competence in dealing with mentally disordered people; must have passed exam set by CCETSW
Application for compulsory admission to hospital or reception into guardianship (Part II)	**Types of application:** emergency (s4); assessment (s2); treatment (s3); in respect of patients already in hospital (s5(1)); reception into guardianship (s7). Application in each case by ASW *or* nearest relative **Summary of procedural requirements:** (see pp 82-84 **Procedure and forms to be used:** see Mental Health (Hospital, Guardianship and Consent to Treatment) Regulations 1983, regs 4 & 5, sch 1
Duty to make application (s13(1))	ASW has a *duty* to make an application in respect of any patient in the area covered by the authority which appointed him
Power to make application (s13(3))	ASW has the *power* to make an application outside the area of the authority which appointed him
Duty to direct ASW to make an application (s13(4))	If so requested by nearest relative, local authority must direct ASW to consider making an application; should ASW decide not to make an application he must give nearest relative reasons in writing
Duty to consult nearest relative (s11)	No application for treatment or guardianship can be made if nearest relative objects (s11(4)); in the case of an application for assessment, ASW must inform nearest relative that he has power to discharge patient (s11(3))

Duty or function and statutory authority	Description
Social reports (s14)	When a nearest relative makes an application, the local authority must direct a social worker (not necessarily approved) to prepare a social report
Duty to interview (s13(2))	Interview must be conducted in a suitable manner and ASW must satisfy himself that detention in hospital is in all the circumstances the most appropriate way of providing the care and treatment the patient needs
Rectification of applications (s15)	If hospital managers agree, faulty application can be rectified within 14 days of admission
Conveyance of patient to hospital (ss6(1) and 40(1))	Duly completed application under Part II gives applicant, or person authorised by him, power to convey patient to hospital within 14 days of date of last medical examination (or in the case of emergency applications within 24 hours of application or medical examination, whichever is shorter) (s6(1)). Hospital order gives ASW power to convey patient to hospital within 28 days of order (s40(1))
Guardianship (s8)	When duly completed application is forwarded to and accepted by local authority, specific powers are conferred on guardian within 14 days of date of last medical examination. (For guardianship orders made by the courts see s40(2))
Transfer of guardianship in case of death, incapacity etc of guardian (s10)	Guardianship transferred to local authority or person approved by authority
Consent to treatment (Part IV)	Social worker (not necessarily approved) may be called upon to give second opinion (s57(2); or may be consulted (ss57(3) and 58(4))
Duty of managers to provide information to patients (s132) and to inform nearest relative of discharge (s133)	Social worker (not necessarily approved) may be asked by managers to undertake either of these duties
After-care reports for Mental Health Review Tribunals (Rule 6, sch 1)	Responsible authority must prepare after-care report for MHRT
Renewal of authority to detain (s20)	Social worker (not necessarily approved) may be called upon for consultation (s20(5))

continued overleaf

Duty or function and statutory authority	Description
After-care and other services (s117)	Local authority and DHA have a duty to provide after-care services for patients admitted for treatment (s3) or under hospital order or transfer direction (ss37, 47 or 48) and then discharged
Application to County Court (ss29 and 10(3))	ASW can apply to County Court to displace nearest relative (s29); or to displace guardian (s10(3))
Warrant to search for and remove patients (s135(1))	ASW can apply to Justice of the Peace for warrant to search for and remove patients believed to be neglected or ill-treated
Powers of entry and inspection (s115)	ASW can enter and inspect premises (other than a hospital) if there is reasonable cause to believe that a mentally disordered patient is not receiving proper care
Mentally disordered persons found in public places (s136)	A constable can take a mentally disordered person found in a public place to place of safety so that he can be examined by doctor and interviewed by ASW
Removal and return of patients within UK (Part VI)	Patient can be taken or retaken, *inter alia*, by ASW (see s138)
Absence without leave (s18) and escape (s138)	Patient can be taken or retaken by ASW
Welfare of hospital patients (s116)	Local authority has a duty to arrange for certain patients in hospital (eg children in its care or patients under its guardianship) to be visited
Offences (Part IX)	It is an offence for a person on the staff of a hospital or nursing home or a guardian to ill-treat or wilfully neglect a patient (s127); and to refuse to allow a patient to be visited or interviewed or to otherwise obstruct person authorised by the Act in the exercise of his duties (s129). Local authority may institute proceedings if any such offence occurs (s130)

APPENDIX III
A DIRECTORY OF
MENTAL HEALTH SERVICES

ORGANISATIONS WITH STATUTORY FUNCTIONS

The Court of Protection
Staffordshire House
25 Store Street
London WC2
Tel 01-636 6877

Government departments
The Under-Secretary of State
The Department of Health and Social Security
Mental Health Division
Alexander Fleming House
Elephant and Castle
London SE1 6BY
Tel 01-407 5522

The Under-Secretary of State
The Home Office
C3 Division
Queen Anne's Gate
London SW1
Tel 01-213 2000

Legal Aid offices
BIRMINGHAM
Podium Centre City House
    (Smallbrook Queensway)
5 Hill Street
Birmingham B5 4UD
Tel 021-632 6541
BRIGHTON
9-12 Middle Street
Brighton BN1 1AS
Tel Brighton 27003

BRISTOL
Whitefriars
Block C, Lewins Mead
Bristol BS1 2LR
Tel Bristol 214801

CAMBRIDGE
Kett House
Station Road
Cambridge CB1 2RF
Tel Cambridge 66511

CARDIFF
Marland House
Central Square
Cardiff CF1 1PF
Tel Cardiff 288971

CHESTER
Pepper House
Pepper Square
Chester CH1 1DF
Tel Chester 315455

LEEDS
City House
New Station Street
Leeds LS1 4JS
Tel Leeds 442851

LIVERPOOL
Moor House
James Street
Liverpool L2 7SA
Tel 051-236 8371

LONDON
29-37 Red Lion Street
London WC1R 4PP
Tel 01-405 6991

MANCHESTER
Pall Mall Court
67 King Street
Manchester M60 9AX
Tel 061-832 7112

NEWCASTLE UPON TYNE
18 Newgate Shopping Centre
Newcastle upon Tyne NE1 5RU
Tel Newcastle upon Tyne 23461

NOTTINGHAM
5 Friar Lane
Nottingham NG1 6BW
Tel Nottingham 412424

READING
Crown House, 10 Crown Street
Reading RG1 2SJ
Tel Reading 589696

Mental Health Act Commission

LIVERPOOL
Cressington House
249 St Mary's Road
Garston
Liverpool L19 0NF
Tel 051-427 2061

LONDON
Floors 1 & 2
Hepburn House
Marsham Street
London SW1P 4HW

NOTTINGHAM
Spur A, Block 5
Government Buildings
Chalfont Drive
Western Boulevard
Nottingham NG8 3RZ
Tel Nottingham 293409

Mental Health Review Tribunal
Regional Offices

	Special hospital in region
Clerk to the Tribunal Mental Health Review Tribunals Hepburn House Marsham Street London SW1P 4HW Tel 01-211 7325/7356	Broadmoor Hospital
Clerk to the Tribunal Mental Health Review Tribunals 3rd Floor Cressington House 249 St Mary's Road Garston L19 0NF Tel 051-469 0095	Moss Side Hospital Park Lane Hospital
Clerk to the Tribunal Mental Health Review Tribunals Spur A, Block 5 Government Buildings Chalfont Drive Western Boulevard Nottingham NG8 3RZ Tel Nottingham 294222/3	Rampton Hospital
Clerk to the Tribunal Mental Health Review Tribunals 2nd Floor New Crown Buildings Cathays Park Cardiff CF1 3NQ Tel Cardiff 825798	

ADVICE & INFORMATION AGENCIES

Citizens Advice Bureaux (CABx)

There are approximately 900 CABx throughout the UK offering information, advice, guidance and support on a wide range of issues. About 250 CABx operate rota schemes staffed by volunteer solicitors, and where appropriate CABx also refer clients to solicitors or law centres. The service is free, and the address and telephone number of the nearest CAB can be found in post offices, council offices and telephone directories.

Community Health Councils

Community Health Councils (CHCs) represent the interests of patients and the public by providing information and advice on local health services, and guidance for individuals who want to make suggestions or complaints. They will also act as a *patient's friend,* and some CHCs will take up a complaint on a patient's behalf. The Community Health Council News and Information Service is based at 362 Euston Road, London NW1 (tel 01-388 4943/4). The address of the nearest Community Health Council can be found in telephone directories, libraries and post offices.

The Children's Legal Centre

20 Compton Terrace
London N1 2UN
Tel 01-359 6251/2 (Advice service 2-5 pm weekdays)
The Children's Legal Centre is concerned with all legal problems as they affect children in England and Wales. It aims to improve children's law through education, research and advocacy, and offers a free advice service.

Mencap (Royal Society for Mentally Handicapped Children and Adults)

123 Golden Lane
London EC1Y 0RT
Tel 01-253 9433
Mencap offers an extensive range of services for mentally handicapped people and their families through its 12 regional offices, 500 local societies and central London office. It supports research into the causes of mental handicap, and runs a specialist bookshop.

MIND

22 Harley Street
London W1N 2ED
Tel 01-637 0741
MIND campaigns to promote the rights of people who are mentally disabled. It offers advice and information on all aspects of mental health, runs courses and conferences, and issues a wide range of publications including **OPENMIND**, a lively bi-monthly magazine.

MIND's Legal Department helps mentally ill and mentally handicapped people achieve their full legal rights and status through advice, information, referral and representation. The staff in the Legal Department have unique experience of issues such as admission and discharge from hospital, consent to treatment, and the civil rights of mental patients. The Legal Department also offers a specialist Mental Health Review Tribunal representation service.

Enquiries to MIND's Legal Department should be made in writing if possible. Legal Department staff are happy to help telephone and personal callers whenever possible, but there is a great demand for the services of the Department and resources are limited.

Enquiries which are not on specifically legal matters should be directed to MIND's Advice, Information and Rights Unit.

National Council for Civil Liberties (NCCL)
21 Tabard Street
London SE1 4LA
Tel 01-403 3888
The NCCL offers advice on issues including complaints against the police, invasion of privacy and discrimination on the basis of race or sex. Written enquiries are preferred.

National Schizophrenia Fellowship (NSF)
79 Victoria Road
Surbiton
Surrey KT6 4NS
Tel 01-390 3651/2/3

Northern Schizophrenia Fellowship
38 Collingwood Buildings
Collingwood Street
Newcastle upon Tyne
Tel Newcastle upon Tyne 614343

North West Fellowship
10/12 Beamont Street
Warrington
Cheshire WA1 1UW
Tel Warrington 571680
These three agencies provide advice, information and support for people with schizophrenia and their families.

The Patients Association
11 Dartmouth Street
London SW1H 9BN
Tel 01-222 4992
The Association offers information and advice about the problems facing patients as consumers.

SCOTLAND

LINK/Glasgow Association for Mental Health
2 Queen's Crescent
Glasgow GH4 9BL
Scotland
Tel 041-332 2541
LINK provides information, advice and counselling on mental health issues. It has a resource centre which develops rehabilitation programmes for former patients.

Scottish Association for Mental Health
67 York Place
Edinburgh EH1 3JD
Tel 031-556 3062

Scottish Council for Civil Liberties (SCCL)
146 Holland Street
Glasgow G2 4NG
Tel 041-332 5960

NORTHERN IRELAND

Northern Ireland Association for Mental Health
84 University Street
Belfast
Northern Ireland
Tel Belfast 28474

PROFESSIONAL BODIES

British Association of Social Workers (BASW)
16 Kent Street
Birmingham B5 6RD
Tel 021-622 3911
BASW is the professional association for social workers in the United Kingdom. It is open to anyone who is professionally qualified or in employment as a social worker. The Association seeks to influence social policy and standards of training and practice in order to improve services for social work clients. It issues a range of publications including the weekly magazine **Social Work Today,** and organises regular conferences and seminars.

Central Council for Education and Training in Social Work (CCETSW)
Derbyshire House
St Chad's Street
London WC1H 8AD
Tel 01-278 2455
CCETSW is an independent body with statutory authority throughout the United Kingdom to promote training for social work in the personal social services. It has responsibility for approving courses and is empowered to award certificates of qualification, to conduct examinations and to carry out research relevant to training.

Royal College of Nursing of the United Kingdom (Rcn)
20 Cavendish Square
London W1M 0AB
Tel 01-409 3333
The Royal College of Nursing of the United Kingdom is the professional organisation, trade union and post-certificate education body for nurses. Over 220,000 nurses and nurses in training are currently in membership. The Rcn Society of Psychiatric Nursing, one of the specialist groups within the Rcn, keeps under review developments in psychiatric nursing practice and studies, and advises on all relevant matters. A new society, the Society of Mental Handicap Nursing, has been set up by the Rcn to provide a similar service for nurses working in the mental handicap field.

The Royal College of Psychiatrists
17 Belgrave Square
London SW1X 8PG
Tel 01-235 2351
The Royal College of Psychiatrists aims to advance the practice of psychiatry and related subjects, to supervise the training of psychiatrists, to promote study and research work in psychiatry and to publish the results. It issues a scientific journal, holds meetings and liaises with colleagues in allied professions as well as acting as a consultative body. The College also holds examinations to institute and maintain training standards, organises scientific meetings and inspects training schemes.